Child Concepts of GOD

by Oliver E. Graebner

Seventeenth Yearbook

1960

LUTHERAN EDUCATION ASSOCIATION

7400 Augusta Street
River Forest, Illinois

Child Concepts
of GOD

by Oliver E. Graebner

Seventeenth Yearbook

1960

LUTHERAN EDUCATION ASSOCIATION
7400 Augusta Street
River Forest, Illinois

Foreword

THE LUTHERAN EDUCATION ASSOCIATION is proud to present the results of a study made by Dr. Oliver E. Graebner, Valparaiso University, the culmination of many years of work in the area of a child's views of God.

The LEA wishes to express its sincere appreciation to Dr. Graebner and to his staff. Special gratitude is extended to the Committee for Scholarly Research of the Missouri Synod for financial assistance. We are indebted to the many children who answered the questions of the instrument "Ideas About God" and to their teachers for administering it.

It is our hope that this publication will enable adults to understand more fully the child's concepts of God, the better to lead him to the arms of our Savior, Jesus Christ.

LUTHERAN EDUCATION ASSOCIATION
Donald Behnken, *chairman*
Editorial Committee

Forest Park, Illinois
May 1960

Preface

IN THE WINTER OF 1954 the author was approached by Dr. Victor Krause of Concordia Teachers College, River Forest, Ill., representing the editorial committee of the Lutheran Education Association, with the request that he undertake a study of the developing concepts of God in children. Having been interested for some years in the rapprochement of Christianity and psychology, particularly in the growth and development of children, he continued his investigation in an attempt to discover new insights in this area, if that were possible. It was felt that the literature was not marked by much more than superficial writing about the more obvious linkage between the two fields and about the development of the God-image in the life and mind of the child. Knowing enough about the problems and difficulties of working in a field of child study which seeks to peer into the life of the mind and the soul to have misgivings regarding the ultimate value of such a study, not to say also regarding competence to undertake it, he was encouraged to attempt the investigation nonetheless.

Since its inception the author has received both moral and financial support for the study from and through the members of the editorial committee of the Lutheran Education Association and from many other persons, especially from Dr. Arthur Miller, executive-secretary of the Board of Parish Education of The Lutheran Church — Missouri Synod.

It seems appropriate in this Preface to recognize also the services of many students at Valparaiso University, notably those of Mrs. Nancy Steffen Kolar, who drew the original sketches for the picture folder, and a corps of some sixty students who gave many hours of painstaking effort in various capacities, as recorders and as clerks to systematize and analyze the data. The author is grateful to the administrative officers of Valparaiso University for granting him a sabbatical leave of absence during the spring of 1957 so that he might devote himself to this project. It is also appropriate to mention the secretarial help and other services provided by Valparaiso University which made this study possible.

OLIVER E. GRAEBNER

Valparaiso, Indiana
Spring 1960

Table of Contents

CHAPTER IV

FINDINGS   32

CHAPTER V

SUMMARY OF FINDINGS   74

List of Tables and Figures

CHAPTER I

Introduction

WHEN GOD FASHIONED MAN of the dust of the ground, form completed, head, torso, legs, arms, and all, He touched him with His breath and man became a living soul. He moved and lived, the creature of God, God's beloved. God gave him a soul and with the soul sensibilities possessed by no other living organism, powers of senses with added powers of understanding and skills to mentally relate impressions received through the senses. Among the perceptions which came upon man was the relationship between himself and all the world about him. He was a person; there was the great world of other-ness (*altera*) outside himself. He and the world about him, including God, would get acquainted with one another.

Adam "became acquainted" by a process of immediate recognition. The process of seeing and identifying what was seen was probably an instantaneous one. He saw Eve, whom God had made, and recognized her immediately as having been created by God out of himself. In their first holy estate as originally fashioned by their Creator, they sensed and understood what they took in with the senses in moments. But after the Fall, all the faculties of man suffered a breakdown, including his powers of recognition, of perception. It became a part of his new mode of life that special effort would be involved to understand what the senses took in. He would now have to more slowly learn what in that first holy estate had come by immediate recognition or mental conclusion. Even as his sensory equipment was imperfect, so also was there distorted and faulty perception. His reasoning was not always logical, his conclusions erroneous. He interpreted experiences at times in an unreal fashion or engaged in making decisions on the basis of faulty or partial evidence. However his ideas, his impressions of himself and others, developed, some true, some faulty, he applied the same processes and skills to all his experiences whether they were sensory, affectional, or religious. His knowledge concerning his Creator was at first immediate, correct, and sufficient. His perceptions of God coincided with reality; there were no distortions. After the Fall, however, his knowledge was disturbed by admixtures of other than accurate ideas; his perceptions became twisted and warped in the direction of his unlawful desires and ambitions. God became smaller and man became larger.

THE CHILD PERCEIVES

What approach, then, shall we take as we view the growing child? What frame of reference will set the direction of our search?

The approach taken by the author is that the sequence of the child's psychical growth may be described as a development from global, generalized impressions of the world without and within himself as initiated by the sense organs, leading gradually through organizing, interpreting, and relating these

11

impressions to one another and to previous impressions. From these generalized, vague, and partially accurate impressions and their generalized but as yet incomplete and fragmentary interpretation there emerges gradually the individuated and differentiated understanding of the world as it relates to the child.

It is hypothesized that at first the child experiences vague, generalized impressions in all his experiences; first come shadowy blobs of impressions, meaningless to him, but sensations which leave their traces somewhere within. Retrospective reasoning leads to this conclusion. From evidence for growth in perception, which is the continual mark of the child's progress, whether at home, at school, or wherever he may be, it is hypothesized that this has been his experience from earliest childhood, in fact, from infancy; and that even as the adult's impressions are at first vague, shadowy, unsure, unclear, and generalized, followed gradually upon closer examination of a new phenomenon by a clearing of the "mental vision," as it were, a configurational wholeness, then an individuated identification and apartness of impressions and meanings, so it is also with the young child. His perceptions of life probably develop from generalized whole impressions, meaningless and unrelated at first, then growing in clarity and relevance with age and experience.

The figure hovering over his bed is at first a shadowy moving mass; then a mass with some uncertain, unclear meaning, having in most cases an accompaniment of pleasant feelings associated with physical care; ending with identification as the mother-figure who supplies comfort — somatic and psychic.

Because of the lack of opportunity adequately to learn at first hand about this developmental process since its most important elements (physiological, biochemical, etc.) are obscure, at least at this writing, we can only infer a process taking place in infancy which is analogous to later life experiences. It is the author's view that such a developmental progression characterizes all of man's earliest learnings, whether they be motor or neuroglandular, mental, social, emotional, or — spiritual. The dawning of understanding the barest notions of muscular co-ordination comes with the maturation of legs and hands and body; the awareness of the effect of person upon person occurs with and is his social awareness; the sorting out, the individuation of emotional experiences, progresses from generalized bodywide experiences which are at first undifferentiated, to particularized, specific, and limited feelings and action.

It would appear logical then to apply the above descriptive analysis also to the evolution of religious percepts and concepts in the child. The child develops a repertoire of shadowy impressions about God — God, the Good One, the Helper, the Provider, the Protector, etc. These are learned through the sensory impressions gained by daily contact with parents and siblings, with teachers and other adults, the details of these perceptions becoming more sharply delineated as he hears and sees and interacts with those who tell him about God. His religious perceptions, his unique, idiosyncratic view of religious ideas are learned through the day-by-day contacts with other humans. When one level of perception and conception is reached in the interaction between the child and his cultural milieu, it serves as a basis for more objective and more discriminating perceptions and conceptions. His religious progression is a part of his general physical, mental, social, and emotional development. His religious perceptions will therefore show a developmental progression in some systematic fashion.

12

THE MATURING MIND

The rationale which underlies this investigation runs as follows: man's perceptual development is related to his earliest impressions in life, impressions which might be termed the product of his sensory experiences coupled with and shaped by the variety of meanings which these experiences produce. As he matures, the child's understandings of the world about him continually alter and shift in accordance with the play upon him by the forces which meet him at every moment of the day and night and by the way in which he responds to these forces and what he does with them. He can see, he can hear, he can taste and smell and feel. Before long, however, he not only is able to see, hear, taste, smell, and feel in some sort of abstract way, but he sees the loaf of bread, he hears the bell, he tastes ice cream, he smells the rose, and feels the fur on his mother's coat. His conceptual and perceptual world is constantly growing and ideas are proliferating. This developmental process, here described, applies with one or two modifications to the life of the soul, the conscience, the life in God.

There is here apparently nothing startling or particularly new. Teachers, formal as well as informal, have always known that the mind of the child grasps more difficult ideas after the simpler ones have been understood, that there is an expectancy for each age level. But, and this need not interfere with a spirit of reverence for things sacred, the insights regarding the processes by which perceptions and conceptions grow, insights gained largely through psychology, have helped clarify and sustain some of our instructional orientation and found relevance in the general understanding of the behavior of man.

It is in keeping with a fair statement of fact that recognition must be made of the limitations of the psychology of perception. It is, as stated earlier, not possible with the means presently at hand to see this process except by indirect methods, that is, by noting evidence for the process. We understand for example that when a child of five years speaks in complete sentences whereas his one-year-old brother talks in one-word sentences, this difference in performance is regarded as prima-facie evidence for actual differences in the ability to speak, to have and to express ideas in word forms. The interpretation of such samples of behavior varies somewhat depending upon the examiner. This is a possible source of error which of course is recognized in all areas of human judgment.

THE SPIRIT OF GOD AND THE SPIRIT OF MAN

The more serious problem which confronts the student of the growing child and especially the child and his religious development, is to know and recognize the limitations of a given method of investigation. Since religion and religious ideas are among the subtlest (at times most ephemeral, at times most enduring) forces in the life of man and since particularly in a Christian orientation there is posited the indwelling of God the Trinity in the body and mind and spirit of the one who believes, the student of man faces the difficult task of sorting out the supernatural from the natural; the mystical and spiritual from the earthy and humane; and the insights and conclusions reached by a child as a normal process of his personal orientation and reorientation toward the events which occur as a result of the fact that he has eyes, ears, etc., from those perceptions which arise primarily from a spiritual source, and of noting the subtle interplay between these two. The mind

13

of man and the Spirit of God combine to produce what are probably unique sensations and unique perceptions. Here there is mystery too deep to know, to understand, but to conclude "O the depth of the riches, both of the wisdom and the knowledge of God."

THE PROBLEM OF THIS STUDY

In spite of the problems of religion in psychology and psychology in religion it might prove profitable for us to look for evidence for ideas that children have about the Deity and His attributes and about our relationship to Him. Wherever their ideas originate, what ideas do they have regarding God and things related to Him? Is there a developmental progression in the growth of concepts in mathematics, in causation, in teleological expectation? This is our problem in the present investigation and this is the burden of the present report.

More particularly, the present writing seeks to answer such questions as the following:

What general ideas do children have about God?

What is the relationship of the home and the ideas about God which a child possesses?

What is the developmental progress of ideas about God through the years?

How is mental level related to ideas about God?

How are religious practices in the home related to religious ideas?

Are there any particular observations regarding religious training and religious ideas of particular religious groups?

ASSUMPTIONS OF THIS STUDY

The following assumptions regarding children's concepts of God form a working background for this study:

1. That a child has ideas about God
2. That these ideas will reflect his cultural milieu
3. That these conceptions of God may be

   a) symbolized

   (1) verbally

   (2) pictorially

   (3) musically

   (4) artistically — by sculpture, painting, drawing, or by a combination of any two or more of the above-listed symbolical approaches.

   b) outside his capacity personally to represent or interpret; this would include those indefinable concepts, percepts, feelings, sentiments — spiritual strivings, which children and adults are capable of, in keeping with their level of understanding and maturity.

4. That concepts are probably related to

   a) age

   b) home

14

(1) parents
(2) religious climate of the home, specificity in or lacking in religion
(3) teaching
(4) practices
(5) siblings

  c) community
  d) ethnic-cultural forces
  e) intelligence
  f) maturity

Children's concepts of God can be ascertained in the following framework, under the following assumptions:

1. We accept the attributes and qualities of God as they are reflected by the Bible as the framework and criterion of knowledge of God, of correct ideas of God.

2. Agreement with and identification by a child of an activity, overt or covert, as including and involving God's intervention, assistance, or anthropomorphic expression, which reflects how God thinks and feels regarding certain situations and events, constitutes a recognition of the attributes portrayed and tacit agreement therewith and thereby implied acceptance of the ideas.

3. While the judgment of the child regarding what he believes God thinks about certain events will reflect in part the attitudes of the child, the present investigation is limited to the disclosure of what ideas or concepts children have of God in particular situations.

4. Pictures of various nonreligious situations or situations having low religious affect and thema will provide opportunities for children to disclose to the examiner how they think of God.

15

CHAPTER II

A Review of Related Literature

THERE IS IN THE PRESENT DECADE a resurgence of interest in the complementarity of religion and psychology. Whereas from the 1920s to the 1940s there was a spirit of mutual suspicion and distrust openly expressed by many on both sides, there is now a greater willingness to frankly examine the orientation and findings of each to the understanding of man, to question and weigh the orientation of each, and to find areas of mutual assistance in the great quest of who man is. Interest in the psychology of religion and religion in psychology is expressed in such books as *Readings in the Psychology of Religion*, Orlo Strunk, Jr., editor, 1959, in which lengthy excerpts on various phases of psychology and religion are presented by 49 different authors on topics from "religious experience" to "methods and research." We need but refer to the "Symposium on the Relationship Between Religion and Mental Health," *American Psychologist*, October 1958, where it is openly admitted that psychologists have omitted a great essential in their work by outlawing religion from their purview. Mention might also be made of the conference conducted by the Religious Education Association in Chicago, March 1957, at which the theme was "The Development of the Sacred Image of Man." Since 1940 the Society for the Scientific Study of Religion has invited teachers, preachers, and writers in the fields of religion and psychology to present papers in areas of mutual concern.

Lest the reader come away with the impression that religious leaders and psychologists and psychiatrists are about to announce a great "agape," bury all hatchets and link arm to arm, it is well to remind one's self that there are still many divergent views of man in psychology, greater in fact than the differences in the viewpoint of man among religious leaders, especially if confined to those working under the general term "Christian religion." Suffice it to say, there is nonetheless a growing interest, tolerance, and willingness to concede where demonstration is strong, as for instance in the work of chaplains in mental hospitals, where teamwork between medicine, religion, and psychology is quite common. It is in this improved climate of acceptability, or at least a climate of tolerance bordering upon sympathy, that this study is taking place.

Empirical Studies. — In reviewing the literature which deals with God in the life of the child the present investigation centered upon empirical studies, passing by the many shelves of books and journals replete with pious thoughts and sometimes platitudinous religionizing which flatters the ignorant into believing they understand and causes revolt among those who put their finger upon shallowness and easy generalizations. It is contended here quite unequivocally that an entry into the field of search for mutuality in psychology and religion requires a degree of courage and care — especially when subjected to print (sic).

Several studies in the literature highlight some of the problems inherent in this sort of investigation.

Patton (25) reported a study on the "Working Concepts of God" held by young people of a rural community. He assumed that "if an idea is so vaguely realized that the holder cannot put it into words it will have little objective reality and value for him." Accordingly, he approached young people 12 to 23 years of age, with a total sample of only 23, with a questionnaire regarding ideas of God. For instance, "Mark the statement G for 'good ways of thinking about God,' F for a 'fair idea,' P for a 'poor idea,' and a question mark (?) for not understanding the item." Items were like the following sample: "God is the heavenly Father; God is nature; God is the Trinity; God is everywhere."

In Patton's investigation the framework of theological orientation has already been established by the statements of the expression used. The respondent rated the statement as "good" or "poor" according to the degree of agreement between the statement and his learned preferences. It is readily observed that here the frame of reference and terminology are fixed. The responses of the child would therefore be in large part an indication of recognition memory, with minimum opportunity for free expression. For these reasons it was determined not to pursue the investigation by this method because it left little opportunity for free expression.

The August 2, 1948, issue of *Life* magazine recorded a children's program emanating from the Dalton School, New York, called "Child's World." In one program children were asked to give their ideas of God. A 7-year-old daughter of a Jewish father and a Catholic mother regarded God as "Moses" — "they built the stone building and well, then God came right on top of it." Douglas, a 12-year-old Episcopalian altar boy, said his first idea of God was someone with "just his head sticking out of the clouds." Billy, a Roman Catholic, was baffled with the way He made everything out of nothing.

In this demonstration there was an attempt to elicit from the children their free expressions regarding God and what God meant to them. It is readily perceived that their expressions about God are reflections of the fusion of their home and church experiences, plus the varying pressures of their cultural milieu.

This method of free expression of the child's imagination regarding what God means to him was investigated by Ernest Harms, who has worked in this area for more than two decades, publishing reports and articles in German and then in American psychological journals. Of particular interest is Harms' study of children's concepts of God by the medium of pictures drawn by children who followed the directive to "draw a picture of God or of the greatest force you know." When they had finished their drawings they were asked to label the picture and to write on the back what it was supposed to portray.

On the basis of criteria which were not clearly reported, Harms categorized the more than 1,000 drawings according to a threefold classification. He is reported to have found that children from ages 3 to 7 depicted God in "fairy-tale" fashion; from 7 to 11 there was "realism"; and during adolescence, "individualism."

The investigation by Harms was apparently carried out with insufficient controls and unclear criteria for categorizing the responses of children. Therefore, while it was an interesting study, it served merely as a point of departure for the present study.

McDowell conducted a thoroughgoing study of the development of the idea of God in the Catholic child, carried through in three parts. Part I was a technical vocabulary test of 12 attributes of God, such as divinity, infinity, eternity, ubiquity, etc., after the author had spent three months interviewing children regarding their understandings about God. This part was therefore a technical terminology recognition test.

Part II was a series of questions based upon the items of Part I; Part III was a group of descriptive terms arranged in such a way that the child might express verbally his notion of God. For example, the child was given four terms: "gentle," "firm," "strict," "stern," and was told to think of God in heaven and to select the word which he felt best described God. A scoring key was developed upon the basis of the judgment of 12 priests.

Upon the basis of the final test of 2,263 children in Catholic schools, both elementary and secondary, in Massachusetts, Missouri, Pennsylvania, Ohio, and Wisconsin, the ideas of children at various age levels were studied. Many interesting observations were noted regarding children's concepts of God. As in Patton's study, the frame of reference and terminology had been set by the author, so that it was still in large part a test of recognition of religious terms.

It is the purpose of the present investigation to secure free responses from the children. Therefore it did not seem advisable to pursue the form of investigation used in the foregoing summaries.

CHAPTER III

Methods and Techniques

SOURCE OF THE DATA

The data upon which this investigation is based come from Lutheran school children attending Lutheran parish schools, from the first through the eighth grades, and represents Midwest United States, including the states Illinois, Indiana, Michigan, Ohio, and Wisconsin. Children are included from the professional and managerial working father down to the unskilled laborer father; from families living in large cities, villages, and rural areas as well. Boys and girls were almost equally divided in the sample, there being a total of 977 cases, with 528 boys and 449 girls.

The information regarding the mental level of each child was secured by asking the examiner, usually a schoolteacher, to affix the most recent intelligence quotient at the top of the questionnaire answer sheet after the child had filled out the questions and turned in the sheets to the teacher. There was no control on the kind of IQ secured, what test had been used, or any other information which would have validated this portion of the personal data. It is understood from the above that this information regarding the respondents' mental level would have to be used with caution and could only be applied along lines of rather wide disparities, high from low, etc. Tables A, B, C, D, and E present the distribution of the sample of 977 cases in the study according to mental level, grade in school, father's occupation, number of years' attendance at parochial school and at Sunday school.

It will be observed that the sample includes the mental level in a range of from IQ 70 to IQ 140 and above. More than one half (56 per cent) of the cases were in the range of 100 to 119 IQ, 18.5 per cent had IQs above 119. An unknown factor is the possible distribution of those whose papers bore no indication of mental level, which number (162) was 16 per cent of the total sample.

Examining the figures regarding grade distribution in Table B the sample includes all elementary grade levels with a predominance in Grades 4, 5, 6, 7, and 8, with Grades 5, 6, and 7 having two thirds of the total.

THE INSTRUMENT

The study was designed to ascertain what ideas and concepts children have about God in particular life situations and to test certain of the hypotheses listed elsewhere as to the nature and origin of these ideas, and factors related to the level of conceptualization. The following procedures were employed in developing the instrument:

1. A list of attributes of God was drawn up in accordance with the Biblical foundation, including Creator, eternal, holy, just, merciful, omnipotent, omnipresent, omniscient, Promise-Keeper.

19

TABLE A
THE DISTRIBUTION OF THE SAMPLE BY MENTAL LEVELS

I. Q.	140+	130—139	120—129	110—119	100—109	90—99	80—89	70—79	Blank
Cases	16	47	133	232	231	116	35	5	162

23%   71%   5%

20

TABLE B
THE DISTRIBUTION OF THE SAMPLE BY SCHOOL GRADES

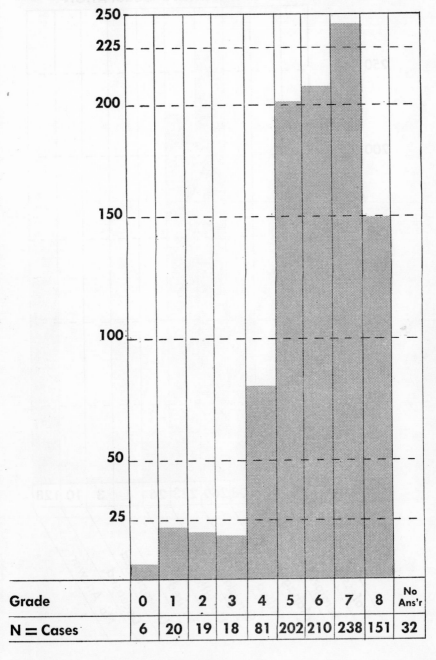

Grade	0	1	2	3	4	5	6	7	8	No Ans'r
N = Cases	6	20	19	18	81	202	210	238	151	32

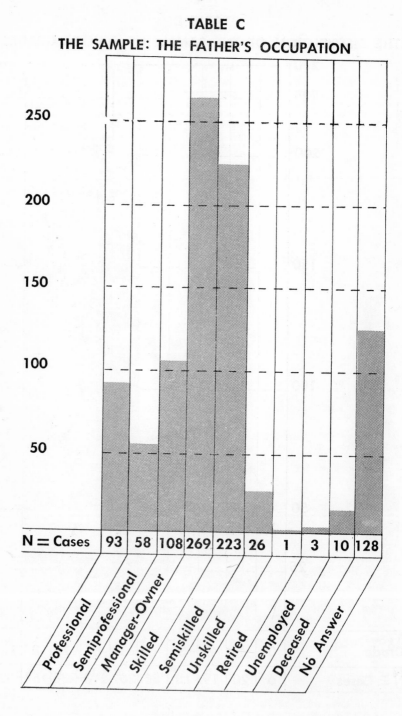

TABLE C
THE SAMPLE: THE FATHER'S OCCUPATION

	Professional	Semiprofessional	Manager-Owner	Skilled	Semiskilled	Unskilled	Retired	Unemployed	Deceased	No Answer
N = Cases	93	58	108	269	223	26	1	3	10	128

22

TABLE D
LENGTH OF ATTENDANCE BY THE SAMPLE AT A
LUTHERAN SCHOOL

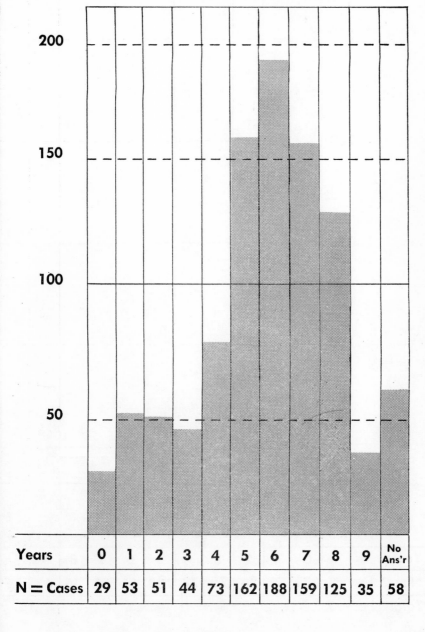

Years	0	1	2	3	4	5	6	7	8	9	No Ans'r
N = Cases	29	53	51	44	73	162	188	159	125	35	58

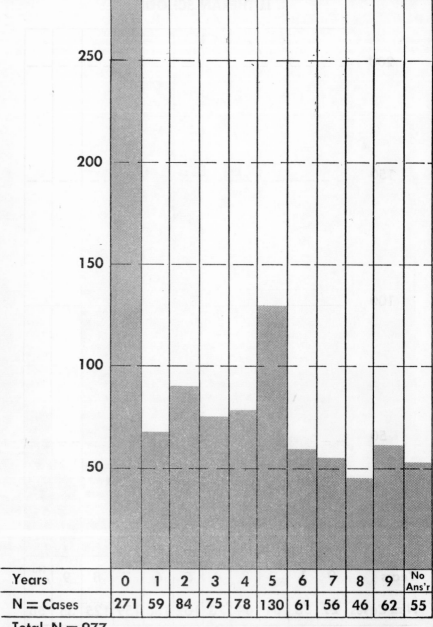

TABLE E

YEARS OF SUNDAY SCHOOL ATTENDANCE OF THE SAMPLE

Years	0	1	2	3	4	5	6	7	8	9	No Ans'r
N = Cases	271	59	84	75	78	130	61	56	46	62	55

Total N = 977

IDEAS

ABOUT

GOD

Inventory by Oliver E. Graebner

Drawings by Nancy Steffen

Boys and girls have many ideas about God, who He is, where He lives, and how He feels about children and their parents and other people.

You will see some pictures in this booklet about boys and girls and older people. On separate sheets are questions about the pictures, namely, how God feels and what He thinks about what is happening.

Answer the questions about each picture which you will find printed on the separate sheets. Do NOT write on this picture book. Write ALL your answers on the question sheets.

There is no time limit but keep working until you are finished. Be sure to look at each picture and answer each question. Be sure to check the number of the question (1, 2, 3,) with the number on the picture.

WAIT UNTIL YOU ARE TOLD TO TURN THE PAGE

1. Is God old like this woman? Why?

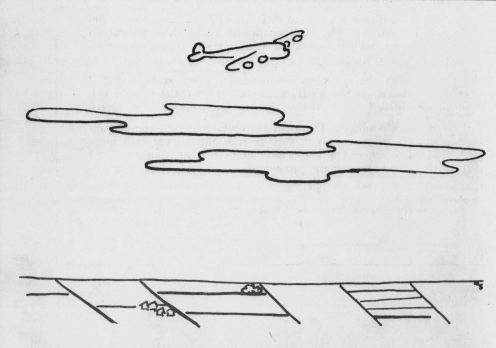

2. Can the flier escape from God? Why?

3. Is God out there in space? What do you mean?

4. Can this boy keep his secret from God? Why?

5. What does God think about this boy?
   Would God punish him if he had done something bad?

6. Where did all this come from?
   How did it happen to be like this?

7. Where did all this come from?
   How did it happen to be like this?

8. What does God think about the boy on the left?

9. Does this picture of an angel remind you of God?
Yes? In what way? No? Why not?

10. What might this man be doing in prison? Why?

11. Will God ever get old like this big tree? Why?

12. Can this man escape from God? Why?

13. What do you think God thinks about what this man is saying?

14. Is God here anywhere? Would He know about the fire?

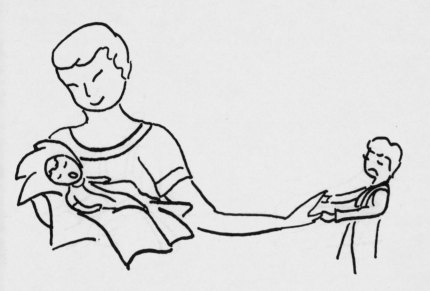

15. What would God do here where the mother is pushing the older child away? What would He say?

16. Is there any connection between God and these squirrels?

17. Make up a short story about God and these two boys.

18. In what way is God like this man?
In what way is He different?

19. Can God catch up with this pilot who is flying a fast plane? How do you know?

20. Where does atomic power come from? What does God think of this?

21. Does God know about this man's need for help?
How do you know?

Here's the bike I promised you.

22. Does God keep His promise? How do you know?

3. Where was God when the baby was growing in the mother before he was born? What was He doing?

4. What is the mother saying?
What would God say if He were there to talk to the girl?

25. Will God ever die?

26. Could God find this man deep down in the ocean?

27. What does God think about the devil?

28. Would God know what the boys are doing?

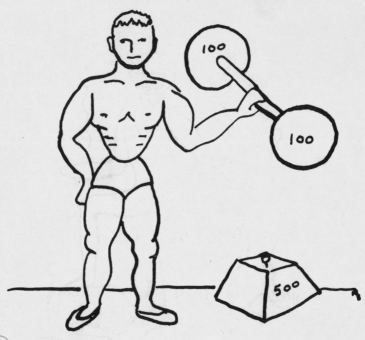

29. How does God feel about this big, strong man?

30. What would God say to this sick girl?

31. Does God have birthdays? How many?

32. What does God think of what this man is saying?

33. What does God think of a boy or girl who has been bad and tries to run away from home?

34. Could God help this boy who is running in front of a car? Explain.

35. If God were not here, would these people behave differently?

36. When there is a storm, how do you feel?

37. What would God tell this boy who is alone in the dark?

38. If God would come to visit these boys at their home, how would He feel? What would He do or say?

2. A number of drawings were made portraying situations related to each attribute given above, situations in life which would involve God's help or knowledge or His regard for man, or His participation in man's life. Questions related to the drawings were also listed, which might arouse the child to regard God's place in the life of man. For instance, using a drawing of an old man, or woman, the question was "How old do you think God is, like this man or woman?" Presumably, if the child thought of God as eternal this would be reflected in his answer.

A total of 44 pictures were reproduced on 4 by 6-inch cards. As a result of preliminary trial the number of pictures was reduced to 38. The general criteria for the selection of these pictures were as follows:

   a) They should be nonreligious: no religious theme or symbolism, no God-reference (except Nos. 9, 10, 27, 30).

   b) They should be situational, portraying incidents common in American life or familiar to American children.

   c) These situations should include nature, old, young, person-to-person, person-to-group, group-to-persons, and group behavior.

   d) These situations should be amenable to combining them with questions which would give the child an opportunity to relate God to the situations and so disclose for the examiner some of his concepts of God.

   e) The projective technique makes possible disclosure of processes (knowledge, beliefs, attitudes) with a minimum of direction or restriction of subject.

SELECTION OF ITEMS

As already indicated above, it was determined to learn about children's ideas about God by using attributes or qualities of God which are commonly accepted by Christians on the basis of Biblical orientation, including Creator, eternal, holy, just, merciful, omnipotent, omnipresent, omniscient, Promise-Keeper. On

25

the basis of this list of attributes pictures were drawn which would give the child an opportunity to answer questions regarding God's relationship (as the child thought of it) to the person or event involved.

The pictures and questions were tried out in a pilot study and amended, eliminated, or replaced as a result of administration by a corps of 12 assistants. After discussing the results in detail, changes were made in the interest of clarity as well as to give the child a better opportunity to reflect his thinking and feeling about God and His relationship to man. The criteria which guided these revisions were, do the questions give the child the desired guidance with sufficient freedom to say what he wishes about God, and are the responses useful in answering the questions inherent in the study?

The instrument now appears in a 20-page printed picture booklet of 38 line drawings under the title "Ideas About God." Children place their responses upon a separate two-page questionnaire. The picture booklet can be used repeatedly.

ADMINISTRATION

Thirty to forty minutes are required to administer the instrument. It has been used with children from 5 to 16 years of age. For young children who are unable to read, it is necessary for the examiner to verbalize the questions for the child and note his responses.

As was indicated in the discussion of the related literature, the problem of method revolved around the question of how to secure responses with the maximum of freedom, yet avoiding leading questions or outright questions of knowledge. It was decided after many trials with a variety of methods to use a combination of the picture-projection method and the questionnaire. The picture would presumably channel the child's ideas into a given area of life, whereas the question regarding that picture would try to elicit from the child how he would relate God to the event and thereby indirectly give evidence to the examiner of how the child thought and felt about God and His relationship to man.

At the top of each question sheet the child is asked to fill in personal information such as age, attendance at church and Sunday school, parents' religious life, father's occupation. There were in all 18 areas of control, with a total of 116 different possible answers, which served as control for the study. The complete key may be found in Appendix Y. When such information as age or sex or father's occupation was sorted with the aid of the IBM sorter, it was possible to relate the answers given to a question according to any of the above-mentioned controls. Thus, it is possible to compare the answers given to a question by 6-year-olds with those who are 12 years of age; or answers given to a question by children of professional fathers with those of unskilled worker fathers.

Directions for taking the instrument are printed on the first page of the instrument (the buff section of this monograph).

TREATMENT OF THE DATA

The first problem in preparing the answers written by the children (or written by adults for the younger children) was to categorize the answers. This was done by reading many samples of the questionnaires in order to note the variety of answers and comments to each question and picture. Then kinds of responses were listed, numbered from 0, 1, 2 through 9. In many cases 0 represented an affirmative answer, with a variety of answers numbered 1, 2, 3, etc., in an unregulated order, while 9 in most instances stood for "no answer" or a blank. For the complete key to responses see Appendix Y.

Similarly, each answer given by a child to each of the 38 picture and question combinations was read and given a code number from 0 to 9 which corresponded to the codes and classifications which had been worked out by the 12 trained assistants. Care was taken to insure the inclusion of the widest variety of answers because this was regarded as the heart of the study. Therefore the resulting key which was used to identify the different kinds of write-in answers as given in Appendix X is complex and cumbersome. Rather than to code the answer as "agree" or "disagree" or "right" or "wrong," a serious attempt was made to keep the original wording or to reflect the sentiment or attitude or idea expressed by the child. Whether this Herculean task of categorizing the responses so that they could be treated quantitatively was worth the effort remains to be seen.

A group of 12 trained readers reviewed each filled-out questionnaire and gave each answer a code number in red pencil to correspond with the keyed answers as described above. Thereafter, each of the controls at the top of each questionnaire was coded in red pencil (See Appendix Z), 0, 1, 2, etc., standing for "mental level," with the range of IQ indicated by the following key:

$0 = 140+$
$1 = 130—139$
$2 = 120—129$
$3 = 110—119$
$4 = 100—109$
$5 = 90—99$
$6 = 80—89$
$7 = 70—79$

After all 977 question sheets from Lutheran children had been coded, this information was transferred to master sheets. From these master sheets it was now possible for the punch-card operator at the Statistical Laboratory at Purdue University to place these coded digits on punch-cards. Thus all personal data as well as the answers given to all questions were translated into code numbers and recorded on IBM punch-cards. Then the data was ready to be processed by the card-sorting machine. The end result was a number of sheets on which are printed the tables which form the data for the quantitative aspects of this study. For instance, cards were sorted for Question Number 20 with the two variables, (1) the varieties of answers given to the question, "Where does atomic power come from?" and (2) the variety of occupations represented by the fathers of those who gave these answers. This enabled the examiner to study such a question as, "Do children of professional fathers have a view about the origin of atomic power different from that of children whose fathers are skilled tradesmen?" Or, using the control of religious observance of the parents, it is possible to study a question like, "Do children of parents who attend church regularly have a different view about the origin of atomic power than those of parents who do not attend church?"

It may be readily understood that it would be possible to secure by means of the sorting machine a matrix of totals in a great variety of combinations. It would be possible to secure distributions on each of the ten different (possible) answers to each of the 38 picture and question combinations, compared with each of the 116 (possible) control items. It became necessary for economic reasons to limit the quantitative analysis of the data to a limited number of questions and controls, as it will be presented in Chapter IV: Findings.

QUANTITATIVE ANALYSIS

Figure 1 represents a sample of the kind of tables which resulted from the comparison of selected questions with a selection of controls. It is a table of raw data and percentages of those who answered this item, distributed along the continuum of one set of controls. The horizontal cells give the percentages of responses according to the controls (age, sex, etc) while the vertical cells give the percentages according to the categories of answers given. In the analysis of data reported in Chapter IV care was taken to check not merely the variations in percentages per se but also in relation to the total number answering a given item.

These tables form the chief means of differentiation of responses of the children to the questions quantitatively.

All tables of percentages of responses were examined by inspection, and where divergencies seemed to warrant it, the significance of the difference between related percentages was found by computing the critical ratio (t-ratio) (see Guilford: *"Fundamental Statistics in Psychology and Education,"* p. 199). The t-test for significance will indicate whether, for example, answers given by boys to a particular picture and question differ markedly from those given by girls (Figure 2).

QUALITATIVE ANALYSIS

The qualitative analysis of the data involved an examination of responses written on the question sheets, for the purpose of ascertaining the thinking and feeling of children regarding the questions and issues raised. By studying the tables of responses both the kind and the number of answers in each category became evident.

It might be well to repeat that this was an empirical investigation, set in a framework of Christian orientation with Biblical reference point as to the nature and qualities of God and His dealings with man. The pictures and the questions were drawn in such a way as to elicit from the children, insofar as possible with these media, responses which would reflect their concepts and perceptions of God. As a result of the pilot studies, only those pictures and questions were retained which (1) gave promise of doing the above, namely reflecting their God-concepts, and (2) would give promise of "correct answers," that is, the picture designed for the eternal quality, for example, should yield responses which reflect knowledge of and reminders of that attribute.

In studying the tables of responses attention was given to the word form as well as to the progression of ideas about God with age and the variations of ideas given by bright children and by the mentally dull. It seemed relevant to

28

FIGURE 1 RELATIONSHIP OF MENTAL LEVEL AND QUESTION 33

("What does God think of a boy or girl who has been bad and tries to run away from home?")

Legend (per cell):
- Percentage of Vertical Column (upper figure, e.g. 8)
- Raw Score (center figure, e.g. 3)
- Percentage of Horizontal Column (lower figure, e.g. 6)

Each cell below is given as: **raw score (vertical %, horizontal %)**; "—" = none.

Mental Level	Responses	He isn't loyal	It is a sin	It's wrong; he shouldn't do it	He should face up to it; take consequences	He should give him a beating	He misunderstood his parents; should stay there	He's running away from God	Don't know	Inappropriate	No answer
140+ (16)	3 (8,6)	3 (—,19)	4 (1,25)	6 (4,38)	—	—	1 (3,6)	—	1 (—,6)	1 (—,6)	1 (—,6)
130—139 (47)	10 (26,8)	8 (5,11)	18 (7,39)	10 (6,21)	1 (16,6)	3 (6,6)	3 (8,6)	—	1 (—,6)	1 (—,3)	3 (3,6)
120—129 (133)	6 (15,2)	14 (13,11)	48 (18,36)	27 (19,20)	1 (16,—)	8 (16,6)	2 (6,2)	3 (25,2)	—	4 (11,3)	17 (20,13)
110—119 (232)	13 (33,6)	33 (31,14)	76 (28,33)	42 (29,18)	1 (16,—)	18 (37,8)	10 (28,4)	2 (17,1)	—	10 (26,4)	34 (40,15)
100—109 (231)	13 (33,6)	28 (27,12)	78 (29,34)	33 (22,14)	3 (50,1)	16 (33,7)	13 (36,6)	4 (33,2)	—	12 (34,5)	3 (3,13)
90—99 (116)	5 (13,4)	14 (13,12)	38 (14,33)	20 (14,17)	1 (16,—)	4 (8,3)	5 (14,4)	3 (25,2)	—	5 (14,4)	20 (23,17)
80—89 (35)	2 (5,6)	7 (7,20)	9 (3,26)	6 (4,17)	—	—	2 (6,6)	—	—	1 (—,—)	8 (9,23)
70—79 (5)	—	1 (1,20)	1 (—,20)	2 (1,40)	—	—	—	—	—	1 (—,20)	—

29

FIGURE 2
T-TEST FOR SIGNIFICANCE APPLIED TO SELECTED ANSWERS
COMPARING RESPONSES OF BOYS AND GIRLS

Question	Answer No.	Boys		Girls		Critical Ratio	d. f.
		N	Per Cent	N	Per Cent		
18	6	112	57	83	42	*2.04	193
18	7	71	59.6	47	39	*2.15	116
18	9	75	59.5	50	39.6	*2.18	123
17	3	190	62	114	37	**4.196	302
20	5	180	34	125	28	1.10	303
23	1	220	42	237	53	2.35	455
23	10	167	32	121	27	.912	286
24	9	111	24	53	12	1.4	162
28	3	79	85	19	73	**3.92	96
9	2	47	9	30	7	.90	75
15	9	83	16	46	10	.98	127
10	1	375	72	294	66	1.66	667

* Significant at the 5% Level of Confidence.

** Significant at the 1% Level of Confidence.

the study to examine a limited number of the 977 cases by the test-and-retest method. A group of 150 children, 25 from each grade, Grades 1 through 6, were selected, who represented a variety of intelligence and socioeconomic background. After an interval of two years these children repeated the same procedure with the same pictures and the same questions. The results were then compared with their first testing. The results will be presented in Chapter IV.

SUMMARY

In answer to a series of questions coupled with 38 pictures, Lutheran children attending Lutheran parish schools in midwest U.S.A. wrote about God as they thought of Him. Their answers were categorized, transcribed to master sheets, again transcribed to punch-cards, thence tabulated according to predetermined combinations of controls and a variety of answers. Tables of responses expressed in percentages were drawn up in order to find out what children think about God and how He deals with man, within the framework of eight personal qualities or attributes of God. Further analysis was possible by means of the table of critical ratios between selected data. Finally, a qualitative analysis of different kinds of answers was made.

CHAPTER IV

Findings

PART ONE

THE HOME AND IDEAS ABOUT GOD

That the home exerts a profound and pervasive influence upon the child's religious life, including the child's implicit as well as explicit religious expression, will not be disputed by the largest majority of the readers of this report. But how the child is influenced, in what direction, and what correlates can be uncovered is still not very clear. It is the purpose of these paragraphs to present evidence regarding the differential effects or accompaniments of religious practices within the home and by members of the family as they relate to specific answers by the children to some of the questions of the instrument. Specifically, can answers be differentiated according to the prayer life of the family? How is attendance at church or Sunday school related to their answers? And finally, are the answers differentiated when sorted against "father's occupation"?

RELIGIOUS PRACTICES AND THE CHILD'S IDEAS ABOUT GOD

Prayers. — In Lutheran parish schools much emphasis is placed upon certain religious observances, notably the participation of the children in public and private prayers. That children will respond to such emphasis and encouragement with varying degrees of compliance and participation is a fact. Here we will be able only to relate the matter of frequency of prayers to the answers given by our subjects; the questions surrounding the "how" of prayer, what kind of prayers are preferred and what kind are offered, and the relationship between kinds of prayers and the child's ideas about God — these are suggestive of and worthy of another study and lie beyond the scope of the present report.

The answers given by the children to the following pictures and their corresponding questions as identified by number were analyzed, namely, 1, 2, 4, 5, 6, 9, 10, 13, 15, 20, 22, 23, 24, 25, 28, 30, 32, 33, 34, 35. These were categorized against the personal data about prayer (Do you pray morning and evening? Yes, No, Sometimes).

It is well to remember in the following paragraphs that comparisons are made especially between answers given by those who claimed they do pray morning and evening with those who do not pray regularly or with those who say they pray "sometimes." Most of the children (79 per cent) claimed that they do pray "morning and evening"; a very small number (3 per cent), that they do not; a limited number (16 per cent), that they pray "sometimes." When the nature of the instrument used in the present study is taken into consideration, plus the general religious orientation of the children here included, it is probably not amiss to hazard the opinion that there were many others, besides those who so indicated, who do not pray very regularly and who are actually in the "sometimes" group. The desirability of being thought of as a regular "pray-er" casts some doubt upon the division in this sample. Interpreted another way, the respondents who identified themselves as praying "sometimes" were probably more honest in this report than were many who marked the "pray — yes" response. It can be stated therefore with reasonable certainty that the "pray — sometimes" were a more clearly differentiated (at least in terms of prayer life) group. Their responses therefore are worth noting.

On Question No. 1, "Is God old like this woman?" the data is represented in Figure 3 and may be interpreted thus: 779 out of 977 pray morning and evening; 467 out of 779 of those who pray morning and evening favored the view that God is different, He is God, eternal, never changing. The rest of the responses were spread over three groups of statements, viz., God is powerful, God is not human, He is a man (anthropomorphism). On the second part of this item in answer to "Why?" answers were in part overlapping, inasmuch as many included or implied the reason for their choice already in answering the original question, "Is God old like this woman?" Forty-five out of the 779 were not sure about a reason for their choice.

A small number, 26 out of 977, who said they did not pray morning and evening identified God as the eternal God or the powerful, nonhuman God. One hundred sixty-four (out of 977) claimed that they prayed "sometimes"; of this number 98, or 60 per cent, stated that God is the eternal One, and small numbers answered in one of the other three ways.

If we turn to Figure 4 we notice the same data as given in Figure 3 but converted to percentages of the vertical sums. In the first column 80.9 per cent of those who preferred to state that God is eternal were in the "yes — praying" group; 1.7 per cent in the "no — not praying" group, and 16.9 per cent in the "sometimes — praying" group. Interpreting this, while 71 per cent of the total number of respondents answered "Yes — we pray morning and evening," and 16 per cent said, "Sometimes," and .3 per cent said, "No, we do not pray," there was no significant difference in the choices of the two (numerically) highest groups. Whether they pray "morning and evenings," or pray "sometimes" about 60 per cent answered the original question, "Is God old like this woman?" in the same way.

In brief, then, it seems correct to say that praying or not praying morning and evening and identifying God as God, the eternal, are not mutually exclusive. This apparently has no bearing upon the question, "Is praying morning and evening related to the child having the idea of eternity in God?"

In Question 2, "Can the flier escape from God?" the tabulations of responses are presented in Figure 5. From this it is clear that the largest number (560) of those (779) who said they pray morning and evening contend that the flier cannot escape from God due to His omnipresence. Another large group (101) give as their reason that God is omnipotent and a third group (83), that God is omniscient.

Looking at the data for the "pray sometimes" group (164 total), 115 of them point out God's omnipresence, 19 His omnipotence, and 17 His omniscience. Converting these to percentages we note that the percentages of the "pray morning and evening" group and of the "pray sometimes" group are virtually the same.

33

FIGURE 3

THE RELATIONSHIP OF MORNING AND EVENING PRAYING AND QUESTION 1

("Is God old like this woman?")

Say Prayers Morning and Evening	Responses	God-Eternal	God-Powerful	God not human	Anthropomorphism	Authority, Bible	Uncertain	Inappropriate	Yes	No	No Answer
Yes	(779)	467 (60)	35	73	33	2	45	16	37	43	28
No	(26)	10 (38)	3	5	1		1	1	1	4	
Sometimes	(164)	98 (60)	8	11	13		9	8	7	8	2

60 — Percentage of Horizontal Column

34

FIGURE 4

PERCENTAGES OF THE RELATIONSHIP BETWEEN MORNING AND EVENING PRAYING AND QUESTION 1
("Is God old like this woman?")

Say Prayers Morning and Evening	Responses	No. God is God-eternal	No. God, powerful	No. God not human	Anthropomorphism	Authority, Bible	Not certain, don't know	Inappropriate	Yes	No	No Answer
Yes		*80.9%	74.4%	81.1%	68.75%	100%	80.3%	64.0%	80.4%	76.7%	93.3%
No		1.7	6.3	5.5	2.0		1.7	4.0	2.1	7.1	0
Sometimes		16.9	17.0	12.2	27.0		16.0	32.0	15.2	14.2	6.6

* E. g. Of those who answered question 1 by saying, "God is God, He is eternal," 80.9% were in the "Yes — we pray morning and evening" group.

35

Again we conclude that whether they say they pray morning and evening or pray sometimes morning and evening is not significantly related to their recognition and avowal of God's omnipotence and omniscience.

That there is no appreciable difference in answers given by children in the study who claim to pray regularly as compared with answers given by children who do not pray regularly suggests that knowledge of God's traits is not a guarantee of regular praying to Him. Here is demonstrated the disparity between faith and life, between Christian knowledge and Christian behavior — even among those reared in a school founded upon ideals of Christian education. It further suggests and emphasizes the need for making personal life behavior consonant with personal knowledge and belief.

knowledge
important

In Question 2 the child is asked: "Can the flier escape from God?" There was agreement by 70 per cent of the respondents in both categories (pray — yes, and pray — sometimes) that God is everywhere present and that the flier could not escape God. Praying in itself did not relate significantly to the answers on this question.

In Question 4 the same holds true. The answers were as strongly in favor of omniscience among those who pray sometimes as among those who pray regularly.

Question 5 pertains to the picture of a boy, an officer, and a judge, and has two questions: "What does God think of this boy?" and "Would God punish him if he had done something bad?" Figure 6 presents the data by sorting against "prayers — yes, no, sometimes." Answers ranged from "God thinks he is a sinner" (211 out of 779), "He should repent" (118), "God will forgive" (94), "God will forgive," "God thinks he should be punished" (30), miscellaneous (172) and no answer (60). The figures here presented in parentheses refer to answers tabulated for the "pray — yes" group. Compared to the "pray — sometimes" group, the responses were not significantly different. It is worthy of mention that this item, Question 5, received a wide spread of different kinds of answers and a large number of "no" responses (82) and "miscellaneous" (172), which latter group was so heterogeneous as to defy classification. It seems that the picture had strong thematic elements, which were reflected in the kinds of responses given. The predominating sentiment favored God's view of this boy as a sinner who would be punished, about one third feeling that God would feel sorry for and would forgive him.

On the second half of this question, "Would God punish him if he had done something bad?" the tabulations showed no significant differences in their choices. Most of them answered "Yes" (unqualified) or "Yes, if he does not repent." About 16 per cent of them said "No." There is no further information which would shed light upon the "No" choices.

In Question 6, God was pointed out as Creator of nature as frequently by children who prayed much or little.

In Question 10, most answers were that the man is merely praying, not that he is praying for forgiveness. In examining the distribution of answers by grade level there appears to be a greater sensitivity of "praying for forgiveness" at the fifth-grade level than before or after; correspondingly, there was a steady increase in percentages with age for the answer, "merely praying," viz., older children said more often "merely praying" than did younger. There

36

FIGURE 5

RELATIONSHIP OF MORNING AND EVENING PRAYING AND QUESTION 2

("Can this flier escape from God? Why?")

"Say Prayers Morning and Evening"	Omnipresence 0	Omnipotence 1	Omniscience 2	Inappropriate 3	No 4	Don't know 5	Yes. Miscellaneous 6	No answer 7
Yes (779)	560 (70)	101 (13)	83 (11)	6	14	3	3	9
No (26)	18	2	1	1	3		3	
Sometimes (164)	115 (70)	19 (11)	17 (10)	3	6		1	
Blank	4							

560 — Raw Score

70 — Percentage of Horizontal Column

37

FIGURE 6
RELATIONSHIP OF MORNING AND EVENING PRAYING AND QUESTION 5

(What does God think of this boy? Would God punish him if he had done something bad?)

Say Prayers Morning and Evening	Responses Total no. of cases	God thinks he should repent	God feels sorry for him	God will forgive him	God thinks he is a sinner	He should be punished	Miscellaneous	No answer	Yes	No	Yes, if he doesn't repent
Yes	(779)	118	82	94	211	30	172	60	6	1	3
No	(26)	1	2	1	9	2	9	2			
Sometimes	(164)	23	7	23	39	4	45	20	1		2
No Answer	4			1	1		2				
Blank	4	1			2	1					

38

was also no significant difference in the percentages of answers by "praying — yes" and by "praying — sometimes" respondents on their choice of answers to Question 10, whether they chose "praying for forgiveness" or "praying — yes."

Again, looking at the responses in Figure 7, it becomes apparent that of those who "pray mornings and evenings," 550 out of 779 said the prisoner was merely "praying," another 10 per cent that he was serving a prison sentence, 31 that he was praying to get out of prison — a total of 591 out of 779 who did not express concern for the prisoner's situation except in superficial terms. Conversely, only 116 out of 779 said that the prisoner was "reading the Bible," "praying for forgiveness," "praying for help in leading a clean life when released," or "praying for God's help." It appears then that the question and picture combination did not arouse anything but superficial concern in the minds of most of the respondents. Could it be that religion is not sufficiently relevant to a great many children?

It appears also that whether a child prays much or little has little to do with his explanation of an incident like the picture of the man in prison. Could it be that the life of prayer in many children from 10 to 13 is too routine to be sensitive to crisis or problem situations?

Question 13 (Figure 8) asks, "What does God think about what this man is saying?" In the picture the scientist in his atomic laboratory is saying, "This is the greatest power in the world." When responses are categorized against the prayer life of the children, these are the results: whether they pray regularly or only "sometimes," 757 out of 779 of the "pray — yes" group and 156 out of 164 of the "pray — sometimes" group said "he is wrong; God is a greater power." Prayer habits were apparently not significantly related to their answers on this item.

Question 15 (Figure 9) reads, "What would God do here where the mother is pushing the older child away?" The answers strongly intimated the sympathy of God for the rejected child. Answers included, "She should love all equally," "Come here, My son," and the Golden Rule. These answers came in equal proportions from children who prayed regularly and from those who did not.

It will be seen from the table that the largest number of responses for all the children to Question 15 was in the very personal relationship category, "God would say, 'Come here, My son,'" and "God would accept the older child." The mother's pushing away the older child is recognized as rejection, as an "unmotherly" act, and as an act which God would not pass by uncorrected. He would certainly personally accept the older child as His child, His son, and would probably, or in any case should, punish the mother for her rejection. Praying has apparently little to do with this view of the situation. The mother has violated a fundamental principle which children readily recognize and condemn. It may be legitimately questioned whether the judgment of children in this instance is more related to religious ideals and practices. In any case, God is pictured as a Rescuer, as a Child-Lover and as a Punisher of one who treats a child ill.

Question 20 has two questions, "Where does atomic power come from?" and "What does God think of this?" The answers to the first question as given in Figure 10 present one of the few differentiations of responses according to the practice of praying regularly or only "sometimes." Seventy per cent of those in the "pray — yes" group said that atomic power comes from God, while 58 per cent of the "pray — sometimes" group said atomic power comes from the ground, from

FIGURE 7

RELATIONSHIP OF MORNING AND EVENING PRAYING AND QUESTION 10

("What might this man be doing in prison? Why?")

Say Prayers Morning and Evening	Responses	Praying for forgiveness Reading Bible	(merely) praying	Serving prison sentence	Praying for help to get out of prison	Help lead clean life when released	Pray for God's help	Inappropriate	Nonsense	Blank
Yes	(779)	94	550	10	31	8	14	35	25	12
No	(26)	6	15	1	1	1		1		1
Sometimes	(164)	25	106		8	5	3	11	3	3

40

FIGURE 8

RELATIONSHIP OF MORNING AND EVENING PRAYING AND QUESTION 13

("What does God think about what this man is saying?")

Say Prayers Morning and Evening	Responses	He is wrong, God greatest power	He is wrong	The man is right	God doesn't like it	Man is not a Christian	He shouldn't — Danger	He doesn't know about God	Thank God for power	Inappropriate	No answer
Yes	752	7	10						2		2
No	22	2	2								
Sometimes	153	3	6								1

41

FIGURE 9

RELATIONSHIP OF MORNING AND EVENING PRAYING AND QUESTION 15

("What would God do here where the mother is pushing the older child away?" "What would He say?")

Say Prayers Morning and Evening	Responses	God would accept all children	God would make the mother suffer	She should love all equally	Come here, my son	He does not like her; He is disappointed	Golden Rule	Man is selfish	Mother must take care of baby	Let him alone	No response	Blank
Yes	(779)	6	9	137	223	58	51	27	14	10	101	143
No	(26)	2	2	3	6	1	1		2		6	5
Sometimes	(164)	2	2	20	53	12	12	3	6	2	22	30

42

FIGURE 10

RELATIONSHIP OF MORNING AND EVENING PRAYING
AND QUESTION 20a

("Where does atomic power come from?")

Says Prayers Morning and Evening Responses	God	The ground; natural causes	No answer
Yes (779)	551 70	148 19	65 8
No (26)	15	3	4
Sometimes (164)	95 58	51 31	17 10

551 — Raw Scores

70 — Percentage of Horizontal Column

43

natural causes, while 31 per cent of the "pray — sometimes" group said it comes from material causes. In this table, therefore, 12 per cent fewer of the "pray — sometimes" group give God credit for atomic power as compared with the "pray — yes" group, and 12 per cent more of the "pray — sometimes" group give nature credit for it. The differences are significant at the one-per-cent level of confidence.

On the second half of the question, "What does God think of this?" (Figure 11) the answers were not clearly differentiated along lines of prayer participation by the respondents. The difference in the proportions of those answering "God thinks it is not good" (30 and 36, respectively) was not significant. Whereas 20 per cent of all the 977 children said that atomic power comes from nature, their answers given to the second question ("What does God think of atomic power?") gave evidence of an involvement by God in the problems of atomic power. This would tend to modify the first interpretation of answers to the first question and the above-mentioned cleavage in the responses according to prayer life. Many feel or think that atomic power comes from nature but that God is interested in and participates somehow in the process.

It is worthy of mention that about a third of the responses expressed strong concern regarding atomic power as reflected in "God thinks it is not good," and similar answers, some with strong thematic elements.

Question 22, "Does God keep His promises?" was answered in the affirmative by all but about .02 per cent of the total number, irrespective of prayer life. In answer to the second part, "How do you know?" 40 per cent of the "pray — yes" group and 30 per cent of the "pray — sometimes" group referred to the Bible as proof that God keeps promises. Praying more often and appealing to the authority of Scripture in this matter seem to be somewhat positively correlated. The remaining answers were scattered and did not suggest any cleavage along "praying — not praying" lines.

It is probably significant to mention that only sixteen per cent of all the children gave their own personal experience of answered prayer as proof for the contention that God does keep promises. Forty per cent of all the children responding gave the Bible as proof.

Whether this latter observation is viewed as illustrating the efficacy of the teaching of the Bible as a reference point in religion or whether in the light of the relatively small proportion of the children who claimed personal experience for belief in God's promise-keeping, it would suggest the possibility of sterility in religious learnings and the compartmentalization of religion. This is a topic for further study.

Question 23, "Where was God when the baby was in the mother before he was born? What was He doing?" gave answers which clearly indicated the omnipresence of God as well as His personal participation in and involvement in the procreative process as typified by such answers as, "God was with the mother and the child," "God was in the baby," "God was giving her a baby." There was no differentiation along lines of prayer life of the respondents. Twelve per cent of the responses read, "God was in heaven" and these would be classified as less appropriate, more limited conceptualizations of God operating in the life of man. For these children God would still be a distant Deity, enthroned up on high, not really very personally involved in and with the lives of men.

Question 24, "What is the mother saying? What would God say if He

FIGURE 11

RELATIONSHIP OF MORNING AND EVENING PRAYING AND QUESTION 20b
("What does God think of this?")

Responses — Say Prayers Morning and Evening	God thinks He wants it this way	God thinks well of it; it is good	God thinks it is not good	God thinks He is greater than atomic power	We don't know	Good if it helps man; evil if it harms man	No answer	Blank
Yes (779)	35	129	236	52	48	124	139	4
No (26)		4	9		3		8	
Sometimes (164)	10	24	59	6	11	15	39	

35 — Raw Score

30 — Percentage of Horizontal Column

45

were there to talk to the girl?" Approximately 75 per cent of the answers to
the first question involved the mother scolding the child for dropping the cookie
jar — "You bad girl," or as berating her, "Why aren't you careful?"

"What would God say?" About a third of the answers concentrated upon
a mild correction, "You shouldn't do such things," or, "Don't do it again." The
answers to these two questions were not differentiated according to prayer life,
but they did show greater confidence in (or hope for) the kindness of God rather
than to expect kindness from the mother in an instance of physical-personal involvement between mother and child.

Question 25, "Will God ever die?" gave responses in an overwhelming
negative and without significant differences between frequently and infrequently
praying children.

Question 28, "Would God know what the boys are doing?" gave responses
with a high degree of agreement and, as in many other questions, with no significance to be attached to answers given by respondents with different degrees of
prayer life.

Questions 30, 32, 33, 34, 35 were all like Questions 25 and 28 in yielding
no significant differences when responses of those praying morning and evening
are compared with responses of those praying "sometimes." Stated in terms of
some of the above-referred-to pictures and questions, whether a child says he
"prays — yes" or "prays — sometimes" does not differentiate God's intervention to
prevent an accident or God's dealings in time of illness or how He feels about
man's boasting of power and accomplishment.

SUMMARY OF FINDINGS RELATED TO PRAYERS

Do children who claim they pray only "sometimes" think of God differently than those who claim they pray regularly? From a review of the questions
included in this portion of the study it seems not; their responses regarding the
omniscience, omnipotence, eternity, affection, and promise-keeping qualities of
God are not significantly different than are the answers given by the regular
pray-ers. To know the attributes of God does not mean that the child will also
pray to Him regularly. Regularity of prayer life as described in this portion of
the report (morning and evening) may or may not accompany knowledge of God's
qualities. The other side of the coin should also be recognized, namely, that if
a child does not pray regularly, this does not mean that he is deficient in knowledge
about God, that the way to get him to pray more regularly is, e. g., to make him
memorize more catechetical facts about God. It cannot be substantiated from this
study that knowledge and worship are necessarily correlative, or that limited
knowledge and worship are antithetical if not mutually exclusive. "I believe
help Thou my unbelief."

SUNDAY SCHOOL ATTENDANCE

In Questions 1, 2, 4, and 6 (see Figures 12, 13, 14) there is a striking
uniformity of answers, regardless of the years of attendance at Sunday school.
This becomes even more noteworthy when the responses of the children who
do not attend Sunday school are compared with either the average of the total
remainder who attended from one to nine years or with any one of the group

46

of "years-of-attendance." There is virtually no difference in answers regardless of attendance at Sunday school. Or to put it another way, the responses are not distinguishable by sorting against years of attendance at Sunday school or against non-attendance at Sunday school. Children who do not attend Sunday school gave virtually the same answers as did children who did attend for varying lengths of time (years).

This might be interpreted in two ways, namely, the education received at Sunday school did not alter their basic beliefs regarding the person and functioning of God, (or)the questions and problems presented in the instrument were not the kind which would give the Sunday school training a chance to function fully. That is, the high similarity of answers might be due to an instrument which is not sensitive enough on specific details or has too low a ceiling, which gave everyone a chance to answer rather "well" and resulted in virtually identical answers.

To counter the argument that the similarity of scores at varying periods of attendance at Sunday school is due to the kind of instrument used, it may be pointed out that there were many different answers to virtually every one of the 38 picture-question combinations. There was a multiplicity of answers and wide spread of scores especially on Pictures (Questions) 5, 10, 13, 15, 20, 22, 24, 27, 30, 33, 38. It is true that the answers were usually concentrated upon one or two thought or word patterns. Yet there was in general much variety and evidence of free expression. This would again appear to support the contention that (1) children wrote what they wanted to write, and (2) that their answers reflected to a high degree what they thought or had been taught about God and man's relationship to Him.

It is recognized that a child who attends Sunday school, with or without accompanying instruction at a Lutheran day school, will receive impressions and religious promptings which would perhaps not be reflected in answers to questions regarding the person and work of God; that there might well be other outcomes of the Sunday school experience which are not reflectd in the instrument used in the present study. Assuming the above as an area for further verification and study, it seems nevertheless pertinent to raise the question which the present study does suggest, specifically, why are the answers so similar, regardless of age and grade, when sorted against a dichotomy of "attendance-nonattendance at Sunday school"?

The lack of significant differences in any of the categories of "attend Sunday school — 0, 1, 2 years" given in the answers, would appear to argue that Sunday school attendance had done little for their God-concepts. Those who did not attend Sunday school gave the same answers (with striking regularity) as those who attended as many as 9 years. Since the religious training of many had presumably been strongly established in the early years in Christian day school, there was little noticeable effect upon their religious thinking for those who also went to Sunday school. This comes as "good news" to those who have not seen the need for children who attend parish schools also attending Sunday school. It would appear to point out the limitations of a one-hour-per-week religious education. But more significant in the present instance is the need for utilizing the Sunday school for other learnings for specialized training, heretofore not utilized or made workable for parochial school children. Would it be ap-

47

FIGURE 12

RELATIONSHIP BETWEEN SUNDAY SCHOOL ATTENDANCE AND QUESTION 1

("Is God old like this woman?")

Attendance at Sunday School, Years	Responses	God-eternal	God-powerful	God-not human	Anthropomorphism	Authority, Bible	Not certain, don't know	Inappropriate	Yes	No	No answer
0	(271)	172 [63]	12	25	14	2	14	6	13	9	4
1	(59)	32 [54]	1	4	6		2	6	3	6	5
2	(84)	43 [51]	5	8	6		5	2	6	9	
3	(75)	38 [51]	3	10	4		4	2	5	9	
4	(78)	35 [45]	6	5	4		9	4	8	8	3
5	(130)	70 [54]	5	22	7		7	1	6	5	4
6	(61)	31 [50]	3	6	2		4	1	2	5	7
7	(56)	36 [64]	5	1	5		1	2	2	1	4
8	(46)	26 [57]	4	2	3		4		1	1	
9	(62)	53 [85]	1	1	1		3	1		2	3

172 — Raw Score

63 — Percentage of Horizontal Column

48

FIGURE 13
RELATIONSHIP OF SUNDAY SCHOOL ATTENDANCE AND QUESTION 2
("Can this flier escape from God? Why?")

Attendance at Sunday School	Responses	Omnipresence	Omnipotence	Omniscience	Inappropriate	No	Don't know	No answer
Years 0	(271)	69 187	15 42	9 24	6	4		6
1	(59)	75 44	6	4		3		2
2	(84)	65 55	15 13	9		5	1	1
3	(75)	72 54	9	15 11	1			
4	(78)	68 53	9	9	4	2	1	
5	(130)	68 89	12 16	13 17		6	1	1
6	(61)	64 39	8	18 11		1		1
7	(56)	71 40	20 11	2	1	1		2
8	(46)	78 36	3	6	1		1	
9	(62)	79 49	5	7				
Blank	(55)	96 53	1	1				

187 — Raw Score

69 — Percentage of Horizontal Column

49

FIGURE 14

RELATIONSHIP OF SUNDAY SCHOOL ATTENDANCE AND QUESTION 4

("Can this boy keep his secret from God? Why?")

Attendance at Sunday School	Responses	Omniscience	No	Yes	No answer
Years 0	(271)	97 263	3	2	3
1	(59)	93 55	3	1	
2	(84)	93 78	5		1
3	(75)	96 72	4		3
4	(78)	92 72	4	1	1
5	(130)	97 126	3		1
6	(61)	98 60	1	1	1
7	(56)	98 55			
8	(46)	98 45			
9	(62)	100 62			
Blank	(55)	98 54		1	

263 — Raw Score

97 — Percentage of Horizontal Column

propriate to use the Sunday school hour for completely different kinds of training and experience for these parochial school children? An objective study of the role of the Sunday school in the lives of Christian day school children seems to be urgently needed.

(margin note: NOT ONLY BUT ALSO!)

FATHER'S OCCUPATION

A selection of questions and answers was statistically treated in relation to the occupation of the fathers. The purpose was ostensibly to see if there was any significant difference in the answers given by children of fathers of different occupational classification.

Referring to Table C, page 22, it may be seen that 12 per cent had fathers who were in the professional class, 8 per cent in the semiprofessional, 14 per cent in the manager-owner, 36 per cent in the skilled, 30 per cent in the semiskilled, and 3 per cent in the unskilled classifications. Apparently the population from which this sample was drawn was more heavily represented in the upper levels of the working population, 34 per cent, than is the generality in the U. S. if the professional, semiprofessional, and manager-owner groups are totalled. This is further underscored by the distribution of the sample by mental ability, as given in Table A, page 20, Mental Level, in which 42 per cent of those answering were in the IQ classification of 90 to 110, and 54 per cent were in the intellectual levels marked "110," and above. This would bear out the description of the sample as above average in mental ability and having fathers who were predominantly in the "skilled" and above groups.

The following questions were sorted against "father's occupation," namely, Questions 1, 2, 4, 5, 6, 9,* 10,* 13, 14, 15, 20, 22, 23, 24, 25, 28, 30, 32, 33, 35. By inspection of the tables of answers given by the different occupation groups it is strikingly apparent that (1) the answers are uniform, regardless of occupation of father, (2) where there is a variety of answers given with no one answer chosen by a majority, of the various groups of fathers, from professional to unskilled, all gave virtually the same answers to all the above-mentioned questions. The t-test of significance was applied in those comparisons which showed a possible significance, but none was found.

The question might be raised at this point, should a greater variety of responses have been expected, a differentiation from low to high occupational grouping, since these differences in occupational groups are marked by certain cultural phenomena?

Apparently the religious education of the children in Lutheran schools, homes, and churches is so uniform and thorough as to produce highly similar answers regardless of the occupation of the father. Stated in another way, the training and work of the father has not produced peculiarities of religious viewpoint, distinct from one another. The son of the doctor answered these questions the same, or virtually so, as the son of the unskilled laborer. In fact, a review of the tables of responses gives one the impression of stereotypy, of striking uniformity of answers irrespective of, among other phenomena in the American scene, the father's line of work. Perhaps it is unwarranted to have expected differences of answers along some sort of gradation of employment of the father

(margin note: F-11)

---

* See Figures 15 and 16.

FIGURE 15 RELATIONSHIP OF OCCUPATION OF FATHER AND QUESTION 9

("Does this picture of an angel remind you of God? Yes? No? Why not?")

Father's Occupation	Responses	Yes. Angels are in heaven, God is holy	Yes, physical likeness. Halo reminds of God	Yes. It is praying	Yes. Reminds of God qualities of divine	No. God is a spirit	Don't know how God looks	God was not created	No answer
Professional (N=93)	36 (39)	8 (9)	11 (12)	24 (26)	10 (11)	3			1
Semiprofessional (58)	11 (19)	4 (7)	8 (13)	15 (26)	4 (7)	5	7		4
Manager-Owner (108)	33 (31)	6 (5)	7 (6)	35 (32)	10 (9)	4	4		9
Skilled (269)	107 (40)	24 (9)	21 (8)	61 (23)	27 (10)	11	8	2	8
Semiskilled (223)	73 (33)	30 (13)	20 (9)	58 (26)	21 (9)	5			9
Unskilled (26)	9 (35)	5 (19)	4 (15)	5 (19)	1	1			2
Retired (1)									
Unemployed (3)	2		1						
Deceased (10)	2	2		4 (21)	2				
No Answer (128)	39 (30)	16 (13)	28 (18)	22 (21)	12 (9)	8			2

52

FIGURE 16

RELATIONSHIP OF OCCUPATION OF FATHER AND QUESTION 10
("What might this man be doing in prison?")

Father's Occupation	Responses	Praying for forgiveness. Read Bible	Merely praying	Serving prison sentence	Pray for help to get out of prison	Help lead clean life when released	Pray for God's help	Inappropriate	No answer
Professional (N=93)	49	46 (33)	31	4	4	2	5		1
Semiprofessional (58)	41	24 (38)	22	6	3	1	1	1	
Manager-Owner (108)	41	44 (38)	41	9	7	1	4	2	
Skilled (269)	51	138 (27)	72 (7)	18 (9)	25	4	7	2	3
Semiskilled (223)	47	105 (30)	67	22	12	4	11	2	
Unskilled (26)		4 (58)	15	2	2	1	2	2	
Retired (1)		1							
Unemployed (3)		3							
Deceased (10)		3	6	1					
No answer (128)	35	45 (39)	50	15	7	5	4		2

46 — Raw Score

49 — Percentage of Horizontal Column

53

since this is probably not marked except in some expressions of attitudes in the general educational life of the child. It remains to be seen whether the uniformity of answers is also observed in other tabulations of results, as, for instance, in respect to mental level.

Those who have taught the children herein studied may feel that whatever impressions about God and God to man were learned by the children over the years, it seems not to have been influenced by the kind of work carried on by the fathers. Would it be fair to raise the questions, "Do fathers affect the religious thinking of their children, at all, or to a marked degree? Is the total life-work motif of the father (which is markedly different in the professional as contrasted with the semiskilled or skilled worker) of so vague and uncertain a character as not to be reflected in the child's mental life?" If this latter is true, it would underscore the remoteness of fathers from their children. It would, however, be unwarranted to use the data analyzed in the present study to do more than raise questions relative to this point, as has been attempted above.

PART TWO

THE SCHOOL AND IDEAS ABOUT GOD

Having treated the findings regarding the relationship between some phases of the home and the child, we turn next to the child at school. It is the purpose of this section of the study to present the evidence for the effect of the (1) grade level, (2) mental level, (3) years in parochial school, and (4) sex, upon the ideas which Lutheran children have regarding God.

Grade Level. — The grade level of a child is probably more highly correlated with his mental age than would be his chronological age. In other words, when considering the child's mental maturity as related to his fellow pupils, his grade placement is somewhat more indicative of his stage of mental development than the age of his years since birth. That this favors the lower limits of mental ability of those who are attending school rather than the upper limits is well known, since children who are "slow learners" are more often carried along from one grade to another and are usually not penalized more than one year, while children of superior mental endowment are more often retained with their age-mates instead of being double- or triple-promoted. The first statement, however, still has a measure of support, namely, that the grade placement of a child gives us a somewhat more accurate picture of his mental maturity than would the mere knowledge of his chronological age. It will therefore be interesting to note how the answers of children on a few of the questions are distributed when sorted by grade in school. Are there any significant differences between children in the lower as contrasted with those in the upper grades? Are there any signs of a developmental sequence of perceptual growth in God-concepts? In order to find some answers to these questions we shall review ten question and picture combinations.

Question 5. "What does God think of this boy?" presents the problem of the youthful offender and the Law. "Would God punish him if he had done something bad?" The sorting of answers along a grade continuum from the first to the eighth grade shows a very high degree of agreement among all grade levels, with highly similar percentages of responses at each grade level to indicate that "Yes, God would punish him if he had done something bad" and "Yes, if he doesn't

54

repent." Almost two-thirds of the respondents answered with an unqualified "Yes" (God would punish him), 14 per cent said "No," and 21 per cent gave a qualified, "Yes, if he doesn't repent." The answers were distributed, as stated above, very evenly over the full grade range. There were no statistically significant differences found in any of the comparisons attempted.

Question 6 asks, regarding a scene in nature, "Where did all this come from?" There were scarcely any who said differently than "God"; eighteen said, "Nature." There were no significant differences between grade levels of responses.

Question 9 reads, "Does this picture of an angel remind you of God? In what way? No — why not?" Most of the answers agreed, "Yes, angels are in heaven where God is holy." Or, "Yes, the halo reminds me of God," or a relationship is implied. In this way almost 80 per cent of the answers agreed that the angel reminded them of God. But 10 per cent said, "No, God is a spirit" and another .03 per cent said they did not know or that God is uncreated.

Children from the first through the eighth grade attribute holiness to angels and to God; for the vast majority this seems to be the dominant point or reminder and similarity between angels and God. Just a small minority chiefly from Grades 5 through 8, about 10 per cent of the total of 977 children in the sample, hesitated or refused to relate the picture of the angel and God with their "Don't know how God looks," or, "God is not created." It is perhaps not amiss to point out the need for enlarging the understanding of the attributes of angels in the heavenly scheme of things, as well as the uncreated "origin" of God.

Question 10 asks, "What might this man be doing in prison?" About one half of the answers indicated that the man was praying for forgiveness, but there were no significant differences in grade levels of responses. There was a higher proportion of the answers in the upper grades, but their actual percentages were not significantly different from the answers given by children in the lower grades. For those who answered merely "Praying" the distribution followed a suggestion of a grade continuum, for example, the proportion of answers given by the children of the first grade (60 per cent) was significantly different from the proportion of answers given by eighth-graders (29 per cent) at the 5 per cent level of confidence. There was a tendency to a smaller proportion of answers of just "Praying" from the children of the upper grades, and contrariwise, a gradually increasing proportion of this same answer from children of the lower grades. There was also some sign of greater maturity in religious thinking among the older children, judging from the greater number (although their total was still only ten per cent of the sample) of answers like the following, "He is praying to get out," "He is praying for help to lead a clean life," and "He is praying for God's help."

Question 11, "Will God ever get old like this big tree?" Fully two thirds of the responses were, "No, God never dies." Of this number, 46 per cent of the 4th graders chose to answer this way rather than to give merely a "No" or another answer. There is here then a clear indication of fuller (and more desirable) expression regarding the comparison of a great tree and God, the older children giving a significantly greater number of answers of this kind than did young children. There was a scattering of other answers but lacking in significance.

Question 14, "Is God here anywhere?" "Would He know about the fire?" resulted in an overwhelming (98 per cent) agreement of answers in the affirmative by all grade levels.

55

[Question 15] "What would God do here where the mother is pushing the older child away? What would He say?" yielded a scatter of answers along the grade continuum from the first to the eighth grade along a very constant pattern, with no significant differences in the answers by the various grades. Children of the lowest grades were fairly sure that God would punish the mother for pushing the older child away; in any event, He would accept all children regardless of age. Apparently, the picture of God as the great Father of mankind and of Jesus as the Friend of children has been well learned.

[Question 18,] "How is God like this man? In what way is He different?" In the scatter of answers to these questions we see the effect of Christian education as it typically affects various age levels in Lutheran schools. Beginning at the second-grade level, and continuing in modest proportions of the total, from 25 to 50 per cent of the answers said that God has a human and a divine nature, or that God was human in Christ. In fact the young children have slightly stronger percentages than the older ones in this direction of answers. About 10 per cent of the answers described the difference between God and man by saying that God is always kind. Like the preceding question, Number 15, the answers to Question 18 clearly demonstrate the effectiveness of Christian education in Lutheran schools, at least in regard to the primary differences between God and man. While there was no reference by picture or question to the second Person of the Deity, there was some indication, as in the present question, of spontaneous reference to Christ when the topic seemed to make this possible.

Answers to the second question of this picture-question combination give further testimony to the above comments. "In what way is God different?" "God is holy, wise, He will not die, He is not limited by a body, He performs miracles." Answers like these were distributed from the first to the eighth grade in fairly regular proportions with no significant differences in grade levels of responses.

Question 20 asks, "Where does atomic power come from? What does God think about this?" Two answers were given, with representative proportions of answers all through the grades in similar numbers, "God," or "the ground — nature." They are not distinguishable by grade level. "What does God think about this (atomic power)?" yielded a variety of answers, the largest total of answers stating, "God thinks it is not good." The next highest number said, "God thinks well of it, it's good," followed closely by "It's good if it helps man; it's evil if it harms man." None of these answers was distinguishable by grade level; where they occurred there was about the same proportion of answers for the various grades represented.

[Question 22] reads, "Does God keep His promises?" The "yes" answers were uniformly in the 95 and above per cent range, with seven answering in the negative. "How do you know?" was answered in a fivefold way, "God is faithful," "God never fails," "God keeps His promises: the Bible has told us so," "He has kept His promises to me," "God has to help others." These can be subsumed under the heading of "proof" by reason of personal experience, by reference to the Bible, by identifying it as a quality or attribute of God, and by reference to man's need. Lutheran children typically give Scriptural references as evidence for God's promise-keeping; this is the most frequently mentioned evidence or proof.

Question 23 concerns God's watchfulness over mother and child, "Where was God when the baby was growing in the mother before he was born? What

56

was He doing?" The localized concept of God removed from earth, up in heaven, during this event, was held by about 13 per cent of the respondents, that God was "in the baby" was the answer of about 5 per cent, that God was "developing the baby" or "giving the mother a blessing" was held by about .2 per cent, that "God is everywhere," by 12 per cent, while the largest number included 47 per cent of the sample who answered, "God was with the mother and the child." In each of these different answers the distribution was, grade-wise, over the full range, with no significant differences in the answers by the different grade levels.

Further elaboration of the findings as they are related to grade in school will be given under the section which deals with "Years of Attendance at a Lutheran Parish School." It will be interesting to note children's responses as they are related to the length of time spent in a Lutheran school.

Mental Level.— There has been more research done in the area of mental measurement of children than in any other in the field of the psychology of childhood. The monumental work of Terman and associates has led to unmistakable, clear-cut conclusions regarding the expectancy for mentally superior children. Not only is their apperceptive grasp more comprehensive and marked by insistent curiosity as well as superior academic achievement, but also their behavior as judged by teachers is marked by social and ethical conduct above the generality within their group.

The questions which call for information and, if possible, definitive answers from the present study might be phrased as follows:

Are there any marked differences in ideas about God among the different mental levels represented?

Do children of superior endowment give evidence of greater curiosity in the religious area; is their religious expression appreciably different from that of the "average-ability" child?

How does our religious training affect the child of low intelligence? Is it suited to his level of comprehension; how does he view God and things religious?

Are there concepts regarding God as reflected in the data which call for revision and change of terminology?

We will first regard the answers given to selected questions and pictures, followed by interpretations of findings.

In Question 1, "Is God old like this woman?" the higher the intelligence, the greater was the proportion who said, "No — God is eternal." In Question 2, "Can the flier escape from God?" there was a similar clear-cut gradation by mental level, the higher the intelligence quotient, the greater the proportion who said, "No — God is everywhere."

In Question 5, "What does God think of this boy?" the need for repentance of the wrong-doer is recognized by all mental levels, with all varieties of answers spread over all mental levels.

Question 9. "Is God like this angel?" The holiness of angels and of God is recognized by all mental levels. There is no significance in the difference between answers of gifted children as compared with slow learners.

Question 10. "What is the man in prison doing?" There was an increasing number of responses as the mental level increased to the effect that the man was merely praying (not "praying for forgiveness," or "praying to get out of prison"). The difference between the percentages of this kind of response when comparing the 90—99 IQ group (70 out of 116, or 60 per cent) with the IQ 140+ group (14 out of 16, or 88 per cent), is significant at the 5 per cent level of confidence. In addition to this fact, the proportions of responses ("merely praying") increased consistently from the IQ 90 up to the top level of mental ability, at each mental level showing an increase. It would appear therefore that the higher the level of intelligence the greater the proneness to identify the prisoner as merely praying rather than relating his praying to God or to his status as a prisoner. It would seem that this failure to see any real religious significance in the situation portrayed indicates a lack of religious insight in a life situation which obviously (in this picture, at least) implied a religious act. Furthermore it is noted that the other responses to this question, "What is the prisoner doing?" answers like "praying for forgiveness," "praying for God's help" were found in greater proportion among those of lower rather than those of higher intelligence.

It might be observed that insight into and appreciation for the religious needs of man are not necessarily dependent upon or correlated with intellectual level, as has been observed by Chassell and Chassell, Maller, and others. It also suggests the need for making religion relevant and vital for all age and mental levels. When considering the great amount of similarity of responses in this investigation generally it is perhaps significant that in such a case as this question and picture (Number 10) there should be a departure from the expected answer, the brighter children giving atypical answers, but answers which incidentally show less religious concern and insight. This leads to the question, is our program of religious education reaching the children of superior endowment as it ought? Is religion for them the living and life-giving source of divine stimulation that it should be for all levels?

It is encouraging to observe that children of all mental levels have learned well the fundamentals of God's attributes and His relationship with men. In Question 32, for instance, "What does God think about what this man is saying?" ("I got this money all by myself"), the answers at all mental levels and especially at the upper extremes of intelligence favor a recognition of God's sovereignty and the need for man's dependence upon Him. The same view is supported by the data for Question 20, "Where does atomic power come from?" The difference in percentages of responses for children with IQ 90—99 (59 per cent), and those with IQ 140 and above (81 per cent) is statistically significant at the 1 per cent level of confidence. Brighter children more consistently gave God credit as the source of atomic power. This incidentally is one of the few clear cases of statistical significance in the comparison of responses. There were only two t-ratios which were significant, one for Question 20 and the other for Question 10.

As one reviews the responses in relation to mental level for the different questions, it is readily observed that there is an increasing number (percentage) of answers favoring a particular emphasis from low to high intelligence. On the other hand, the reverse is true for a few items where the percentage of answers increases as one descends from high to low intelligence.

Questions whose answers show a tendency toward an increase or a decrease in relation to intellectual level: 1, 2, 5, 9, 10, 15, 20, 24, 25, 28, 30, 32, 33, 34, 35.

Twenty questions show an increasing tendency in the frequency of responses from lower to higher levels of intelligence to certain answers.

E. g.: Question 1 — omnipresence of God
       Question 2 — omnipresence
       Question 5 — justice
       Question 9 — holiness
       Question 10 — forgiveness
       Question 15 — love
       Question 20 — Creator
       Question 24 — justice and love
       Question 25 — omnipotence
       Question 28 — omniscience
       Question 30 — omnipotence
       Question 32 — Creator
       Question 33 — merciful
       Question 34 — omnipotence
       Question 35 — Creator — love — family

(I. e., the brighter the child, the larger the number of preferences for a certain answer.)

Seven questions show an increasing tendency in the frequency of responses from upper to lower levels of intelligence to one kind of answer (i. e., a greater proportion of low intelligence children preferred these answers than did children having higher intelligence)

E. g.: Question 5 — justice
       Question 9 — holiness
       Question 15 — love
       Question 20 — omnipresence
       Question 24 — justice — love
       Question 34 — omnipotence
       Question 35 — Creator

Figs. 17 and 18 illustrate this distribution. Fig. 17 illustrates the increase of percentages from low to high intelligence, and Fig. 18 shows the reverse trend for other items. There appears to be evidence for the following generalizations related to the kind of answers given, when sorted against mental level: (1) There is much more preponderance of preferences among children of higher intelligence than among lower, that is, many more of the mentally above-average children agree on the answers to be given to questions than do those below average. (2) There is a gradual and almost uniform increase in the proportion of preferred answers on certain items, from low to high intelligence. (3) There are a few reversals Fig. 18 (cf.). (4) These trends are not restricted to particular attributes of God, but are more directly related to the problem posed by questions and pictures.

For example, in Question 5, "What does God think of this boy?" (boy standing before a judge and an officer) there was an increasing number from high to low intelligence who answered, "God thinks he is a sinner" and "God thinks he should be punished." God appears as the punisher of evil — but also the One who forgives the repentant sinner.

Again in Question 20, "Where does atomic power come from?" the largest percentages favoring the answer, "From the ground" (or, from natural causes), were among those in the lowest intelligence levels. It might also be indicative

59

FIGURE 17
PERCENTAGES OF RESPONSES TO SELECTED ANSWERS RELATED TO INTELLIGENCE

I.Q.	Attributes of God													
	Omnipresent: Q. 1 (0)	Omnipresent: Q. 2 (0)	Holy: Q. 9 (0)	Creator: Q. 20 (0)	Creator: Q. 32 (0)	Creator: Q. 35 (0)	Omnipotent: Q. 25 (1)	Omnipotent: Q. 30 (1)	Omnipotent: Q. 34 (0)	Omniscient: Q. 28 (0)	Loving-merciful: Q. 10 (0)	Loving-merciful: Q. 15 (2)	Loving-merciful: Q. 33 (2)	Just: Q. 24 (1)
140+	63	94	51	81	63	75	94	31	63	100	88			75
130—139	68	79	52	87	49	70	81	32	57	98	85	43	38	85
120—129	62	74	50	75	47	72	92	32	58	98	70	15	36	75
110—119	63	74	49	72	37	70	93	28	50	95	69	19	33	72
100—109	59	64	45	58	30	64	89	26	45	92	67	19	34	75
90—99	58	66	43	59	29	62	84	22	41	91	60	15	33	78
80—89	54	51	40	51	37	54	80	25	34	89	69			60
70—79	40					60								

FIGURE 18

PERCENTAGES OF RESPONSES TO SELECTED ANSWERS RELATED TO INTELLIGENCE

I.Q.	Attributes of God						
	Justice, Q. 5	Holy, Q. 9	Loving-justice, Q. 10	Creator, Q. 20	Justice, Q. 24	Omnipotent, Q. 34	Creator, Q. 35
140+	13	25	6	18		12	18
130—139	28	26	8	8	4	13	17
120—129	26	36	12	18	10	12	14
110—119	25	37	13	19	16	14	17
100—109	30	38	14	25	18	18	19
90— 99	33	30	16	22	25	26	20
80— 89		20	17	37		14	20
70— 79							20

of the general orientation of those in the lower mental levels that they also had the largest percentages of those who answered, "God thinks it is not good" (atomic power).

In Question 24, "What does God think of the girl?" (who spilled the cookie jar) those in the lowest mental levels had the largest number indicating "I don't know."

Length of Attendance at a Lutheran Parish School. — The question to be considered in the next portion of the report is whether the answers given on a selection of items in the picture-question instrument are differentiated along lines of the number of years that a child has attended a Lutheran parish school. Would the answers of the child who had attended many years show marked differences from those given by children who had attended but a few years?

Questions 1, 2, 4, 5, 6, 9, 10, 15, 18, 22, 23, 24, 25, 27, 28, 30, 32, 33, 34 were examined with the following results; Figure 19 presents sample data for one item, Question 1, "Is God old like this woman?" sorted against years of attendance at parish school. The largest percentage of children at each year level gave the answer 0, "God is God, eternal, never changing." The remaining six answers are scattered among children of varying years of attendance. Beginning at the fifth year a larger proportion (.16) of those choosing answer 0 were represented; this held true for year 6, 7, and 8, as well. It will also be noted that the larger proportions under responses 1, 2, and 3 were likewise found among those who had attended Lutheran school 5, 6, or 7 years. An increase in years of attendance seems to be related to a greater tendency to identify the eternal, the manifest divine qualities of God. At the fifth year this difference seems to become more marked. This observation is also made regarding questions of the study numbers 3, 4, 5, 9, 10, 13, 15, 18, 22, 23, 24, 25, 27, 28, 30, 32, 33, and 34. In other words, all questions of the instrument presently under study show the same tendency — answers are more widely differentiated from inappropriate to appropriate, from theologically immature to mature among younger or older children or among those with fewer years of parochial school education than among older and those with five or more years of attendance. Beginning at about the fifth year level answers show greater uniformity and incidentally also greater understanding regarding the qualities of God as commonly conceived by Christians.

The etiology of this difference along a years-of-attendance continuum can only be conjectured in the present study. The difference is probably due to one of five factors, or, due to a combination of these, namely, (1) peculiarities of the instrument, (2) peculiarities of the sample of children, (3) inherent differences in the perceptual grasp of children at different age-grade levels, (4) the effect of teaching method, (5) the effect of longer attendance at Lutheran school. Let us consider these possible factors in the order given.

The peculiarities of the instrument would hardly be an important factor in producing the differences in responses among children who had attended parish school one to four years, as opposed to responses from five-year-and-more respondents, because the question samples form a broad basis for ideas regarding God, and the generality and uniformity of responses for one question after another would strongly suggest a search for the reason elsewhere. Parenthetically, it may be stated that the instrument and the results do not identify cause or causes, they

62

FIGURE 19

RELATIONSHIP OF YEARS OF ATTENDANCE AT PARISH SCHOOL AND QUESTION 1

("Is God old like this woman?")

ATTENDANCE AT PARISH SCHOOL — Years	God as God, eternal	God — powerful	God — not human	Man — anthropomorphism	Authority — Bible, pastor	Not certain, don't know	Inappropriate	Yes	No	No Answer
0	13	3	1	3	2	1	3	3	1	1
1	24	2	6	4	0	1	3	4	8	1
2	20	3	5	3	0	2	2	6	9	1
3	19	1	2	2	1	2	1	3	10	3
4	29	1	12	2	0	8	4	6	9	2
5	93	9	19	5	1	5	2	15	5	8
6	112	12	17	12	0	13	8	3	3	8
7	104	8	12	10	0	14	2	2	4	3
8	97	4	9	5	0	4	1	2	1	2
9	23	2	2	2	0	2	1	0	2	1

merely present the evidence for children's religious ideas. They may suggest areas for further study or suggest possible causation.

The second possible factor is the sample of the children. Table B, page 21 presents the sample by grade and here it is clear that the sample does not include what might be reasonably expected in a random sample, since the grade levels include the following totals, Grade 1: 20, Grade 2: 19, Grade 3: 18, and Grade 4: 81. However, Table D, page 23 presents the sample by years of attendance at parochial school and here the distribution is quite different:

Years	Number of Children
1	53
2	51
3	44
4	73

The total number of children in the category given above is 25 per cent of the total number of children who answered this portion of the question data sheet. Since the respondents lived in a widely spread geographic distribution it would appear that their answers could be regarded as fairly representative of children with their respective "years of attendance at parochial school." A comparison of the spread of the sample as given above will reveal that more than one half of the children included in the "years of attendance at parochial school" in the year 1, 2, and 3 groups were not necessarily the same persons as the sample by grade (1: 20, 2: 19, 3: 18) but were presumably older children who had attended parochial school but a short period of time. It is therefore not warranted to state that the difference was due primarily to immaturity, since various age levels above the usual ages for children in Grades 1, 2, 3, and 4 were included.

The fourth possibility is the effect of teaching method. If the results of the various questions are spread over a wide variety of children but showing marked uniformity of answers as the years of attendance at parochial school increase, and if it is doubtful whether this is due to peculiarities of the instrument or due to the sample, it would seem to be worth looking at the method of teaching as a possible causal factor.

When the data are studied it is evident that the children in the sample have learned well the basic concepts of God as reflected in their verbalizations regarding the qualities of God. Beginning at about the fifth year of attendance awareness of the relatedness of God's qualities to the life of man takes on more mature significance. They show more clearly a grasp of the attributes of God and are better able to apply this sensitivity and conceptualization to the relationship between God and man than their younger siblings and some older ones who had not attended parochial school as long as they. Before the five-year-attendance level there appears to be much greater diversity of answers, which demonstrates more dramatically either conceptual precocity or stupidity, as the case may be. Some children of six and eight years give answers which show insights and understandings far in advance of their age-grade mates and some show quite the reverse. At about the fourth year of attendance at parochial school (which may or may not coincide with fourth grade, as far as the present data is concerned) answers begin to be more uniform and in general more appropriate and demonstrating greater understanding of God-concepts. However, a problem arises when an attempt is made to account for

64

the similarity of answers at each year-of-attendance level. Children who have attended one, two, three, or four years give a wide spread of answers; whereas at the fifth year and above, they show great uniformity, almost stereotypy, of answers. Does something occur after about four years of religious study to produce uniformity which did not happen before this time? *Conf. Instruction?*

From the above it seems necessary to give attention to (1) the development of desirable concepts at each age-grade level in keeping with the conceptual level of that age and not to expect too much from the immature, nor to expect too little from the more mature; (2) the uniformity, the tendency toward stereotypy, of answers especially by children in the upper grades, or among children who have attended parish school five years or more, would appear to invite further investigation. Among questions which call for answers are the following: Is the teaching of religion in the Lutheran schools so "pitched" at about the fifth grade level that those below this grade-year level have difficulty in relating God to their life beyond the learned repetitions of catechetical statements and terms and prayers? Is religion so taught that those who are above the fifth year in parochial school are offered little in the way of ideas and motivation to enlarge their understandings beyond "5th year" religion? The present study seems to imply a need for an honest look at the facts of religious education at the primary level and its effect upon the religious thinking of the growing child.

PART THREE

SEX

The distribution of answers by boys were compared with those given by girls for twenty-five questions, but the results were not marked by more than a few signs of cleavage along sex lines. While many comparisons were made, many standard errors of the difference in percentages were computed to test for significance, only a few were found to be significant. In a sweeping generality it may be said that as far as the items in this instrument are concerned, the scores yielded but a very few real differences between the way boys answered the items and the way girls answered them. This strongly suggests that in our society Lutheran boys and girls have highly similar viewpoints about things religious, including concepts of God and God-man relationships. The corollary which suggests itself is to the effect that there are no special problems of appreciations, understandings, or attitudes which boys and girls have in our part of the world, which might produce special problems for the teacher of religion. Girls do not apparently have an edge on boys in their religious intuitiveness; boys are likewise not in a superior, advantageous position. It also suggests that the teaching which these children have received has not favored one sex more than the other.

The teaching of religion in Western society is usually directed to man in general, with no special emphasis or concern for the sex of the learner. Problems of man's nature, his nothingness in the sight of God, the need for God's grace, and other basic matters of religious concern are taught as a rule to classes of boys and girls with the assumption that those who can hear and read, can understand enough under God's guidance to effect the changes which would make and prove them to be Christians — that this occurs irrespective of sex; that the Scriptures as the chief guide in matters of faith and life lay no burden, utter no threats, and make no promises for boys which are different from those which might apply to girls. The teaching of religion can therefore be identical for both sexes. No particular attention need be given in this respect for either boys or girls. This general assumption, which has been the framework of Christian teaching, is supported by the overt expressions given on the instrument used in the present study. Lest the present paragraph appear to be presumptuous, let it be added that it is recognized that God needs no study of children, psychological or historical, by direct questions or by pictures or by any other method to become effective in the life of the child; nor are the present observations regarding the lack of cleavage of answers to the questions of this study to be interpreted as a unique discovery. Perhaps its contribution, if any, lies in its general support of the present method of religious instruction and its pointing to a lack, apparently, of sex differences per se in the child's understanding of religious concepts. Where there are differences in conceptual framework or conceptual impressions in children, this would be due to factors other than sex.

A word of caution is here in order. The present investigation and the results may be used first and foremost in the study of one segment of the child population in the United States, Lutheran children who attend a Lutheran school primarily in Midwest U.S.A. Such matters as sex cleavage might show up quite differently if a similar study were made of children, for example, in Mexico, or Haiti, among the Eskimos, the Ubangi, the Hindus, or natives of New Guinea. Perhaps cultural differences in child-rearing would reflect different concepts of boys toward God than those of girls.

A final question would seem to be warranted. Are the responses of the boys and girls in the sample of this study affected by the cultural variations of child-rearing in the United States? Not long ago many parents were advised to guide their children by an indirect system of extreme permissiveness. Many held on to an "old-fashioned" method of "rodding" rather than "sparing." In the present decade parents are often advised to bring up their children by a system of discipline somewhere between the extremes of permissiveness and authoritarianism. The children of Lutheran parents, at least the largest segment of those included in the present sample, appear to fall in the latter category of "parenting." For the most part middle-class to middle-and-upper socio-economic-educational class, they would include the variations of by-the-book, and by-the-rod, methods of child-rearing, with probably a greater proportion leaning toward permissiveness. The children of such a variety of parents have not in the present instance reflected sex differences in reaction to authority or succorance, human or divine. Religious teaching seems to be effective as regards concept-formation irrespective of the kind of rearing experienced. Whether the above-outlined interpretation would be substantiated by a thorough study of parent practices and child behavior as related to beliefs is uncertain and suggests another question for further study.

PART FOUR

PICTURES LIKED MOST AND LEAST

At the end of the question sheets which children filled out in this study there were two questions, "Of all the pictures in this booklet, which picture did you like the most? Of all the pictures in this booklet, which picture did you like the least?" Following the procedure commonly employed in projective tests, the respondents were asked to indicate their preferences for "most-liked" picture and "least-liked" picture by writing the numbers of their choices on the questionnaire sheet. Having worked their way through a variety of 38 pictures and their respective sets of questions, they were at the end asked to indicate their preferences.

The chart below presents the scatter of preferences for Pictures 1, 4, 6 dichotomized by sex. The purpose was to learn about their preferences per se, and to learn about sex cleavages, which might possibly be reflected in their choices.

The pictures "most liked" are as follows, in a descending order of preference:

> Picture 9 (angel)
> Picture 10 (prisoner)
> Picture 7 (nature)
> Picture 35 (family)
> Picture 23 (mother and child in arms)

The pictures "liked least" were as follows:

> Picture 27 (the devil)
> Picture 32 (the rich man)
> Picture 17 (boys, "I hate you")
> Picture 28 (stealing)
> Picture 15 (mother pushing the child away)

The chart presents the five pictures receiving the highest number of choices as *"most* liked" and the five pictures receiving the highest number of choices as *"least* liked," with the percentages of responses by boys and by girls for each picture. An inspection of this table shows a concentration of choices for the "most liked" and for the "least liked" strongly favoring one picture for each kind of choice, Number 9, the picture of an angel, as the "most liked," and Number 27 the overwhelming choice as the "least liked," the picture of a demon.

MOST-LIKED PICTURE			LEAST-LIKED PICTURE		
	Per Cent of			Per Cent of	
Picture No.	Boys (521)	Girls (444)	Picture No.	Boys (518)	Girls (443)
9	20*	24	27	35	35
10	8	6	32	6	7
7	6	6	17	6	6
35	3	10	28	5	5
23	5	3	15	3	6
Total percentages 42		49	Total percentages 55		59

It will also be noted from the chart above that there were no appreciable or significant differences in choices between boys and girls. The five pictures included in the chart were most frequently chosen by 42 per cent of the boys, and by 49 per cent of the girls.

The pictures in order of preference have been identified above. Included in the "most-liked" pictures is Number 10, the praying prisoner. This was probably

---

* Percentages rounded

selected by many because of the implied need for succorance and the prisoner's very act of praying. Number 7 is the scene from nature, while the last two selections of "most-liked" were Number 35, the happy family scene, and Number 23, the mother and child-in-arms picture. Besides these choices there was a wide scatter of preferences for each of the remaining pictures save three. Their numbers were all small.

In addition to Picture Number 27 (the devil), the four other pictures receiving the next highest number of "least-liked" choices were Number 32, the rich man, Number 17, the boys playing, one saying "I hate you," Number 28, the boys stealing, and Number 15, the mother pushing the older child away. Here greed and hate are identified as strongly negative qualities, in addition to the personification of evil, the devil. Among the pictures most liked there was a wider variety of situations chosen, including, besides the personification of goodness, an angel, a repentant prisoner, a scene from nature, and the family setting of parents and children.

By negation or by omission, the respondents did not choose (as "most-liked") pictures of air or sea travel, atomic research, firemen at rescue work, the promised bicycle, the strong man, birthday parties, or a rich man and his pile of money.

The selection of the pictures of angel and devil as "most-" and "least-liked" of all the pictures by approximately half of the children in the study is very likely (1) a reflection of their religious education, and/or (2) a reflection, in part, of the general effect of such an instrument as this upon children who are already well oriented in formal Christian education. For many readers the selection by the children here indicated will come as evidence to support the view that religious education in the long run pays off in its total impact upon the growing child, for thereby, they would say, he is enabled to make the wise choices when alternatives are offered. Others might contend that the general tone of the questions and their constant "God-reference" has a tendency to develop, as the child proceeds from question to question, a mental (and spiritual) attitude or set which ineluctably results in the selections described above — the contrast between good and evil. The fact of the matter is the selection. Also it may be pointed out that the majority of responses dealt with primary issues of life, God, God-to-man relations, man-to-man relations, and least with ephemeral wishes, desires, and needs. It would appear therefore that it is safe to conclude in favor of (1) above — that the selection of the "most-" and "least-liked" pictures does reflect in large part the effect of their religious education. Why the selection of angel and devil, for instance, as the examples of good and evil was not made by a much higher percentage of children is a matter for further speculation and study.

PART FIVE

ANALYSIS OF VARIED ANSWERS *

The reader will recall from the description of the instrument used in this study and the manner of treatment of the data that the answers of the children were categorized by frequency under each question. Each picture and its corre-

---

* Cf. Appendix Y.

sponding question was originally planned to portray an attribute of God. The actual responses of the children at times fulfilled the expectancy (identified the attribute of God) and at times reflected other ideas suggested by the pictures and questions. The responses for the various questions as they are related to the attributes of God are next inspected for whatever information may be gained regarding the fundamental question of this study, what ideas do children have regarding God?

Analysis of Typical Answers. — Summarizing the analysis of varied answers as represented in the category key, a number of observations seem to be pertinent.

1. God, the God of the Bible, of catechism, and of theological description is nearer to the child than God the personal living force or essence. This seems to be the oft-repeated impression. God is the all-knowing, all-powerful One, who forgives repentant sinners, but He is really a watcher, not too close to man, rather vaguely engaged in direct and personal relationship with man.

It is within normal expectancy that where the religious education of children rests upon a body of memorized quotations and religious statements it would require an added step in teaching (and learning) for the child to relate these truths to himself, to his personal life. This underscores again the imperative need for making religion relevant to the child at his age level, of building upon the theological model a world of application so that God is God, God in the heaven of heavens, infinite, immutable, yet concerned about man, His creature, personally involved in man's life. That the child at an early age should make God over in the image of man (human features and qualities) is in part a problem of semantics and in part a problem of spiritual and mental maturation. But that somewhere in his years of religious education he should gain the impression of and belief in Him as his God, his Friend, closely, personally, "in whom we live and move and have our being" — this must happen or our religious teaching has failed in its most important task.

2. There is a tendency toward confusing the "omni-qualities" of God. The eternal quality is at times identified with all-powerful, or all-knowing, or all-present, or each of these is confused with one of the other qualities. That this should occur at the younger age levels is a reasonable expectancy. Probably the more important indication which may be drawn from this is that the sovereignty of God is recognized by children of all grade levels and by many below the first grade in school, and that this sovereignty, this concept of God-above-and-over-all is verbalized by one child as "He's everywhere," by another, "He's the greatest power on earth," and by a third, "He knows everything." The growth of basic concepts of God's attributes in children calls for more investigation, since for instance the confusion of the concepts described above is reflected by the responses, but whether this confusion is a function of age, of Lutheran teaching practices, or of some other factor is not clear in the present study.

3. Of all the attributes sampled in this investigation children identified the creative function of God most clearly and frequently. That God is all-powerful and that He punishes evil are probably next in frequency of mention. The mercy and kindness of God follows in third place. Could this apparent sequence be the direct result of teaching of Law and Gospel, in that order? That this succession coincides is apparent. Whether there is a causal relationship between these sequences is another question not directly answerable by the data.

A question which might intrude upon the reader at this point is whether for pre-school and first- and second-grade children it would be wise to emphasize this sequence in the teaching of man and God and their relationship, settling heavily upon God as the Just One and man as the damned one, God as the Punisher of evil and man as the enemy of God, before applying the grace of the Gospel. For children who are being reared by God-fearing and God-loving parents and teachers, who are in a state of grace through Baptism — these need encouragement to consecration, piety, and godly worship through the greatest teaching possible — of God's grace and forgiveness and the life under grace which lies open to them. Admittedly this requires recognition of human imperfection, "the nothingness of man," the all-sufficiency of God on the part of the teacher, first of all, but the tender years need all the evidence of love which believing parents and teachers can bring to them, rather than to first pound them to pulp through severe teaching and preaching of the Law. Perhaps it is well to take a lesson from God's approach to the child — "come unto Me" — "be baptized" — the first approach of God to the child is His grace, His love, not hate, or rejection. Later as the child's knowledge of the world about him, including himself, becomes clearer, he must also know the full assessment of life, his life, his sin, and the reconciliation of the irreconcilables in God and Christ.

PART SIX

A REVIEW OF RESPONSES FROM 150 LUTHERAN CHILDREN, 25 AT EACH GRADE LEVEL, GRADES 1 THROUGH 6, TO A SELECTED NUMBER OF TEST ITEMS

Question No. 5

    A. "What does God think of this boy?"

    All grades agree that the boy had been "bad," up to the fourth grade, where the opinion that God still feels love for the boy is expressed by approximately 50 per cent of the respondents.

    B. "Would He punish him if he had done something bad?"

    All first graders agree God should or would punish this boy; in Grade 2 approximately 50 per cent thought He would not. In Grades 3 and 4 the major opinion was that God would punish the boys. In Grades 5 and 6 the majority thought God would punish the boy only if he did not repent of his sins.

Question No. 8

    "What does God think about the boy on the left?"

    Grades 1 to 3 agree that God forgives the boy because He knows the boy is sorry and thus receives God's love and forgiveness, but they also express opinions to the effect that (4th) the boy should be punished, (5th) that the boy should ask forgiveness, and (6th) that the boy is not really sorry and was not being very polite when he pushed the other boy down.

70

Question No. 9

"Does this picture of an angel remind you of God?" "In what way?" "Why not?"

All grades up to and including Grade 4 liked the picture because it reminded them of God for various reasons: in all grades they were reminded of God because they felt the angels live in heaven or because the angels are God's helpers. In Grades 2, 3, and 4 they were reminded of God because the angels appeared to be praying. Those who were reminded of God by the picture in Grades 5 and 6 were for the most part reminded of His holiness and the angel's holiness. However, in these two upper grades there was a great distribution of "no's" ascribed to God's omnipresence and His everlasting nature. In the fifth grade there was also a large number who "did not know what God looked like," and for that reason answered the question negatively. In the sixth grade many answered both "yes" and "no" because (1) God is holy, (2) God doesn't have wings, or, God is a Spirit.

Question No. 10

"What might this man be doing in prison?"

The first three grades agree that the man is praying, but only in Grade 1 do they go on to say that he is praying for forgiveness. Grade 4 brings in the idea that the man is praying for forgiveness and "to get out of jail." Grade 5 brings in a wide diversification of answers of opinions already expressed and then brings in the thought that the man is asking God to get him out of prison whereupon he will become a new man — a propositional measure. Grade 6 agrees for the most part that the man is asking God's forgiveness for the wrong he has done.

Question No. 15

"What should God do here where the mother is pushing the older child away?" "What would He say?"

Grades 1 and 2 felt that God was sorry for the boy and would punish the mother. Grade 2 especially expressed the opinion that the mother did not love the boy and that God would take the boy with Him. In Grade 3 the opinion that God loves everyone equally is first expressed and gains strength in each of the succeeding grades. Also, in Grade 3, the idea that God would punish the mother diminished in frequency and continues to do so in the succeeding grades. In Grade 5 the idea that "God will help the mother love both her children equally" takes root and continues into the sixth grade. Grades 5 and 6 also express the opinion that perhaps God's causing some harm to come to the rejected child will make his mother love him.

Question No. 20

"Where does atomic power come from?" "What does God think about this?"

Grades 1 and 2 are diversified as to whether atomic power comes from God or man. In Grade 1 all agree that it is "bad because it hurts people," while Grade 2 brings into light the opinion that "God thinks it is all right if it doesn't hurt people." Grade 3 seems to be a combination of these opinions. In Grade 4 many did not answer either part. Those who did answer agreed that atomic power comes from God, but when asked what God thought about it, the answers were either "very good" or "very bad." Grades 5 and 6 also agreed that atomic power comes from God, but they expressed the opinion that it was good only if it was used right.

In none of these questions was the question of sex of any importance, that is, the answers were not distinguishable by a sex dichotomy.

Question No. 23

"Where was God when baby was growing in mother?" "What was He doing?"

Most of the answers here were pretty general, placing God either in heaven or with the mother, protecting both the mother and the baby. Quite a few had an adequate understanding of God's relation to the growth of a baby. A significant number did not answer this question at all or said they did not know how to answer it, showing perhaps a hesitation to talk about the growth of a baby in his mother or a lack of information on the subject. Those who answered, answered quite well.

Question No. 27

"What does God think about a devil?"

The answers here were rather uniform, identifying the devil with evil, sin, meanness, etc. The most important trend was towards an increasing identification of the devil as the source of sin, as the children increased in age. At first they just used adjectives to describe the devil and then gradually began to name him as the cause of sin. A few said that God would still love the devil, and quite a number gave the devil human attributes and connotations.

Question No. 30

"What would God say to this sick girl?"

This question had two aspects — the fact that the girl was sick and the question of what her parents would say if she died. The answers, therefore, were somewhat ambiguous and confused, but there were some definite trends nevertheless. The first-graders answered that either God would make her well or would take her to heaven; they did not treat the aspect of the parents. The second-graders were of the general opinion that she would get better and some of them made mention of prayer to obtain help. The third-graders begin to mention both aspects of the question and come out with the general opinion that God will take care of both parents and children. By the fifth grade the answers are more stereotyped, such as "don't worry," "just pray," etc., and they begin to think more of the possibility of dying. The sixth-graders talked in great majority of heaven and eternal happiness and the child being with his parents in heaven.

72

Question No. 32

"What does God think of what this man is saying?" (miser)

On the whole the children had a little trouble with this one in that so many went around the basic problem that "God provides and all thanks must go to Him." Many of the smaller ones became bogged down worrying about where he got the money and consequently accused him of stealing it. Many were of the opinion he must have robbed a bank. The first- and second-graders knew something was wrong but could not quite put their finger on it. They thought the man should give his money away. The third- and fourth-graders did not have much to say about "giving it away" and they started to apply such terms as "selfish" and "miser." In the fifth grade the phrase "idol worship" appeared several times and they began to mention that God helped the man. The sixth-graders understood the sovereignty of God.

Question No. 33

"What does God think of a boy or girl who has been bad and tries to run away from home?"

The answers to this question show a definite progression. The first-graders answered quite simply that God would think this bad. The answers of the second-graders feel that God will continue to love the child in spite of his sin. In the third grade the children begin to feel a certain responsibility to their parents and the fact that their parents will forgive them. The fourth-graders go one step farther and sense that they should ask forgiveness and that God as well as their parents will be willing to forgive. The sixth-graders showed a strong consciousness of sin and an angry God. A significant number said that repentance is necessary but along with this come stereotyped answers, such as "he should turn to God," "he should repent of his sins."

Question No. 35

"If God were *not* there, would these people behave differently?"

The great majority of the children answered this question with a "yes." Very significant were the answers of the first- and second-graders who had a very definite understanding of the evil that would result if God were not there — being frightened, being sad, fighting and general discord. One little boy defined "sin" as "tearing up the Bible." The third and fourth grades were not so expressive in their answers, and the fifth and sixth grades showed definite signs of previous learning by often evading the question with answers such as, "But God *is* there." By this age, it was not so easy to conceive of a world without God, and they would not dismiss Him with such a simple statement.

CHAPTER V

Summary of Findings

RELIGIOUS PRACTICES AND THE CHILD'S IDEAS ABOUT GOD

Prayers. — Whether a child prays regularly mornings and evenings does not seem to be significantly related to his ideas about God's attributes, eternity creative power, etc. He may or may not pray regularly and have clear or faulty ideas about God. Regularity of prayer life appears not to be a mark of either advanced or of immature ideas about God. The question about atomic power as an example, resulted in some agreement and some contradiction, for those children who prayed regularly were more prone to give credit to God for atomic power; the "pray — sometimes" group was more inclined to attribute this to natural causes, with no mention of God by name. This would appear to support the thesis that regular prayer life will also involve more God-involved thinking in the child, at least in the sort of situation presented in this instrument, or in the question regarding atomic power and its origin. It will be noted (p. 44) that many feel that while atomic power comes from nature, God is interested in and somehow participates in the process.

Another finding is that praying more often and appealing to the Bible as the proof that God keeps His promises is somewhat positively related.

We remind ourselves that prayer is a fruit of faith, evidence for the in dwelling of God in the life and soul of the believer; that prayer in childhood begins probably with voiced repetitions of learned prayers and religious ter minology, "God" and "Jesus," etc. That God the Holy Spirit utilizes this means along with Baptism, to work faith in the heart of the child and to move him to pray in faith to God. Praying in itself, especially as regards the frequency of praying, seems not to have significant relation to particular ideas which children have about the qualities of God like eternal, all-powerful, Keeper of Promises many of those who pray less regularly have, at least on the verbal level, very similar ideas about God as those who pray regularly.

Sunday School Attendance. — Answers by children in Grades 1 through were categorized according to attendance in Sunday school. It will be recalled that the sample in this study is composed entirely of children who then were enrolled in Christian day school. Out of the total of 997 children, 29 per cent indicated that they did not attend Sunday school, while the remainder attended from one to nine years. When the table of statements made by children of various years of attendance at Sunday school is compared with answers given by the non-attenders, there is striking uniformity of answers. There is virtually no difference in answers on a large sample of questions in the instrument regardless of attendance at Sunday school. Children who do not attend Sunday school gave virtually the same answers as did those who attended Sunday school for varying lengths of time, up to nine years.

74

The above finding seems to invite further examination of this finding and suggests a review of the place of the Sunday school in the life of the child who attends Christian day school, including curriculum, program, etc.

Father's Occupation. — An inspection of answers given by children in the sample whose fathers were employed in occupations from unskilled to professional, with a predominance in the skilled and higher group, reveals that (1) the answers were uniform, regardless of occupation of fathers; (2) where there was a variety of answers (with no single answer chosen by a majority) this dispersal of answers was found in all occupational groups. While the t-test for significance was applied in many apparently promising comparisons, no significant difference was found on the basis of occupation. There is no gradation of answers or trends of concepts in keeping with the difference of occupation of father, from laborer to professional.

THE SCHOOL AND IDEAS ABOUT GOD

Grade Level. — When the answers for most of the questions in the study were reviewed along a grade-continuum, it was found that similarity of answers at all grade levels was the rule rather than the exception. Many tests of significance were applied to pairs of percentages of answers by children of higher and lower grade levels on the same question(s) with no significance found. Here and here a trend was noted, for instance, in Question 10, "What might this man be doing in prison?" There were some signs of greater religious maturity in religious thinking among the older children, judging from the greater number of more mature answers given, although this number was still but a small percentage of the total. In Question 11, "Will God ever get old like this big tree?" from the fourth grade on there was clearer indication of fuller and more desirable expression of God as Creator of nature.

In Question 18, "How is God like this man? In what way is He different?" we see the full effect of Christian education in Lutheran schools coming to the fore, because from the lowest to the highest grade level there was clear evidence of knowledge about the essential difference between God and man. There were no significant differences in grade levels of responses. These truths were taught early and children learned them at an early age; once learned, they were reflected along the entire grade-level continuum.

There seems to be a need among Lutheran children to learn better and more fully the attributes and functions of the angels in the heavenly scheme of things. The ministry of angels to the lives of children is apparently not very effectively learned by Lutheran children. *close relationship with man.*

Mental Level. — Children of higher intelligence agree more consistently about answers to be given to a number of questions in the study. A greater proportion of those of higher intelligence recognized the eternal and omnipresent attributes of God. But there was a failure to relate religion to life, as for instance *for to the heart* in Question 10 (man praying in prison), among those of higher mental ability. Children who had lower intelligence quotients related the picture of the prisoner to religious ideas more consistently than did the higher. *nearer to the heart*

There seems to be reason for doubting whether our religious education in the elementary grades is reaching children of superior mental ability as it ought.

75

Too many among them answer questions with memorized answers or with less originality and relevance than did many of appreciably lower mental level. An exception is (p. 60) the finding that bright children more consistently gave God credit as the source of atomic power.

Years of Attendance at Parochial School. — Younger children and those with fewer years of parochial school education gave answers which were more immature and inappropriate than did older children, with a noticeable improvement and consistency of answers, beginning at about the fifth year of attendance at parochial school. Underscored is the need for teaching religious concepts in keeping with the perceptual grasp of each age-group level.

Sex. — No significant difference in responses was found with respect to sex. Lutheran boys and girls have highly similar religious concepts. Religion may well be taught without particular concern for one or the other sex.

The cultural effect was not noticeable in comparing boys' and girls' answers. Choices of "most-liked" and "least-liked" pictures were not distinguishable by sex. Girls did not select pictures essentially different from boys.

Child's View of and Relationship to God. — In several questions (5, 8, 15, 17 — questions which deal with how God feels about people who have wronged others) the dominating theme of the responses is one of God's love for sinners, forgiveness, compassion, and acceptance of all children. In certain questions (8 and 38) the responses of happy, sad, etc., to questions which deal with how God feels about certain situations seem to indicate that the child ascribe to God human emotions and thinks of Him as a remote watcher who is pleased or displeased, rather than as a God who has a direct, forgiving relationship to men.

In Question 33 (a boy running away from home) one finds that the variety of answers given tends to emphasize the wrong of the boy rather than the forgiveness of God. A possible reason for this may be training. Picture (a boy before a judge in court) is more removed from everyday life, and since God is often depicted as a judge, the theme of forgiveness is more readily suggested. Pictures 8 and 17 (play situations) occur commonly, with adults frequently reminding the child to show love and forgiveness. Whereas Picture 33 is only moderately related to everyday life, it is forbidden through implication presented merely as a "don't" (without reference to forgiveness).

ATTRIBUTES OF GOD

Eternal. — In response to Questions 1, 11, 18, 25, 31, dealing with the eternal character of God, the answers given often refer to other attributes such as omnipotence, holiness, or kindness — or, the answer may indicate a confusion between Christ's earthly life and death and God.

Omnipresent. — This attribute, although confused on some occasions with omnipotence or omniscience, appears to be evident to the child in Pictures 2, and 12 which show pictures of "space," sky, or large areas. However, in Question 38 (a boy alone in a storm) the quality of omnipresence is not as strongly suggested (for in this question the reference is made only to "you" and "storm, not to God as in the other questions) as it is in Question 37, where the question refers to God's telling the boy something.

Omnipotence. — This attribute was not clearly evident in the picture

76

In Questions 13, 20, 27 the phrase "what does God think about—" suggested to the child an attitude toward the object in the picture such as right, wrong, bad, should be punished, rather than God thinking of His own power. Question 19 suggested omnipresence as well as omnipotence. Question 34, a question closer to everyday life, received a variety of responses—none of them referring to the abstract idea of complete direct power; some referring to an indirect method of helping—making the driver stop, telling the boy to watch; others considered God's power to be limited.

Just.—In Questions 5 and 24 which indicate the child committed a wrong, the responses fall into 2 general categories; those which thought that God viewed the person as a sinner, or that he should be punished; and those that thought God would forgive, or that the person repented.

Creator.—Questions 6 and 7 suggest that God or nature made the scenes depicted in the pictures. (The similarity of these responses is probably due to the fact that the questions were closely related through order.) Question 16 likewise suggests God's role as Creator and Preserver; Question 23, although less precisely, also suggests God as the source of existence. However, Question 29 (How does God *feel*—) again suggests an attitude toward the man rather than a reference to an attribute of God.

Mercy and Kindness. — In questions 8, 33, and 38 (questions asking how God thinks or feels) God's attitude toward the persons is expressed. In Question 8 some indication of God as forgiving is given. In Question 10 God is regarded as forgiving and helping. In Question 15 the responses again fall into two general classifications—those regarding God as a lover of children, especially the neglected; and those that regard Him as a punisher of the evildoer.

Holy.—The picture of the angel suggests heaven where God is; the halo and the folded hands also suggest God to the child, since these references are frequently made in early childhood training.

Anthropomorphism.—This type of response occurs to Questions 3, 11, 18—questions referring to the eternal character of God. In Questions 3 and 18 the responses appear to be directly suggested by the pictures and the questions which ask for similarities between an old woman and God and between an old man and God.

Confusion Between God and Christ.—The questions in which the child confused God with Christ are those relating to the eternal character of God (18, 25, 31). God was like the old man because He has a human nature; God can die because Jesus died on the cross; God does have birthdays at Christmas—His age being represented as that of Christ. In Question 18 the picture of the old man suggests the similarity between the most obvious characteristics of the man, his human nature, and the human nature of Christ. The word "die" in Question 25 perhaps suggests Christ's death on the cross. The word "birthday" in Question 31 easily suggests Christ's birthday at Christmas.

QUESTIONS AND TOPICS FOR FURTHER STUDY

As usually occurs in making a study, more questions are raised or suggested than are answered. The present study is no exception. The following are a few of the many areas and topics which seem to call for further investigation:

1. How are child preferences for prayers related to their ideas about God? It may be hypothesized that prayers are the reflections of their God-concepts.

2. At what age does the relevance of religion to children begin and when does it break down? Are we doing a better job of teaching religion in the primary grades or in the upper elementary grades?

Praying much or little seems to have little to do with relevance of religion or the lack of it among children. Is this really so?

3. How relevant is religion in the life of the child? How effective is our teaching? Only 16 per cent of all the 977 children gave their own experience as proof that God does keep His promises; 42 per cent referred to the Bible as proof. Have the religious or other life experiences been so dull or so intellectual that religion does not touch them personally? Is our teaching sterile, is it compartmentalized? *rational? Not completed? Concrete x abstract.*

4. Are the judgments of children regarding the mother's pushing the younger child away from her (Picture 15) more related to general cultural practices of parent-child relationships in the U. S. than to religious ideals and practices?

5. May we generalize upon the finding that children showed greater confidence in the kindness of God than in the kindness of man (Question 24)? If this is supported by another study, it is hypothesized that children have keener insight in some areas of religion than do their elders.

✓ 6. What values lie in the attendance at Sunday school for the child who also attends Lutheran day school? Does he gain little more than the opportunity to contribute the knowledge which he already has from the parish school classes? Is there a need for a special Sunday school program for Lutheran school children? If there is, what would its nature be, how might it function, what outcomes might be expected?

7. Do fathers affect the religious thinking of their children? Is there any significant difference in the religious thinking of children according to the occupational level of the father?

In the present study no difference was found in the answers of children of fathers who are in many different occupations. Is this lack of difference due to the cultural remoteness of the father, due to the "effectiveness" of religion teaching which allows no variation, or to other factors?

8. What can be done to make religion interesting and vital to children of superior mental endowment? May we expect greater religious insight and appreciation from them than from those of lower endowment? Is religious insight related to the level of intellectual endowment?

9. Is religion so taught in Lutheran parish schools that those below the 5th grade have difficulty in relating religion to their daily life beyond catechetical quotation? Is religion taught on the fifth grade level and little beyond?

10. Is the development of religious concepts affected by and related to child-rearing practices? Do children who are reared in an authoritarian home develop religious concepts typical of their experiences, while those from highly

permissive homes develop a different set or attitude toward life, God, man, and religion?

11. How personal or impersonal is the God-concept for children of different age levels? How does age relate to personal involvement with God?

12. How do the responses of children who have not attended parish school ✓ but have attended Sunday school compare with the responses in this study? Is the finding of the present study that parish school children who do not attend Sunday school give answers which by and large are not significantly different from those given by parish school children who do also attend Sunday school — is this finding substantiated?

A study of family life and its religious life as they affect the religious thinking of the child.

13. To what extent, at what age, do children identify "God" with Jesus Christ? When does the concept of the Trinity become operative?

14. Are the findings of the present study peculiar to Lutheran children or are they identified also in other Christian groups?

Bibliography

1. Amers, Edward, *Psychology of Religious Experience*, Boston: Houghton Mifflin Co. 1910.

2. Allport, Floyd H., *Institutional Behavior*, Chapel Hill: University of North Carolina Press, 1933.

3. Blaine, Harry Elmer, *The Biblical Knowledge of High School Pupils*, Typewritten A. M. Thesis, University of Chicago, 1920.

4. Bovet, Pierre, *The Child's Religion*, New York: Macmillan Co., 1929.

5. Chassell, C. F. and Chassell, L., "A Test of Religious Ideas Involving Ranking of Selected Answers," *Religious Education*, January 1922.

6. Conklin, Edmund S., *Psychology of Religious Adjustment*, New York: Macmillan Co., 1929.

7. Dimock, Hedley S., *Rediscovering the Adolescent*, New York: Association Press, 1941.

8. Dresser, Horatio W., *Outlines of the Psychology of Religion*, New York: T. Y Crowell Co., 1929.

9. Gesell, Arnold and Ilg, Frances L., *Infant and Child in the Culture of Today*, New York: Harper and Bros., 1943.

10. Greene, Katherine Glass, *The Evolution of the Conception of God*, Boston: The Christopher Publishing House, 1934.

11. Gruen, Werner, *Religionspsychologie*, Breslau: Hirt, 1926.

12. Guin, Howell, *The Use of the Idea of God in Materials Prepared for Seniors by the Methodist-Episcopal Church*, Typewritten B. D. Thesis, University of Chicago, 1940.

13. Harms, Ernest, "Die Variabilität der Individualpsyche als Grundlage des Verstehens des religiösen Menschen," *Zeitschrift für Religionspsychologie*, VI (May 6, 1931), 214—238.

14. Harms, Ernest, *Die seelische Struktur des religiösen Menschen*, Leipzig: Ungelenk, 1932.

15. Harms, Ernest, "Religionswissenschaftliche Bewertung der modernen National Religionen bei Skandinaviern und Balten," *Proceedings of the International Congress of Anthropology and Ethnology*, London: Institute for Anthropology, 1943.

16. Harms, Ernest, "Über eine neue Art und Verwendung von Tests," *Schweiz. psychol. Rdsch.*, No. 102 (August—September 1930).

17. Harms, Ernest, "The Development of Religious Experience in Children," *American Journal of Sociology*, L (1944).

18. Hartshorne, Hugh, *Childhood and Character*, Boston: Pilgrim Press, 1919.

19. MacLean, August H., *The Idea of God in Protestant Religious Education*, New York: Teachers College, 1930.

20. Maller, Julius Bernard, "Character and Personality Tests: A Descriptive Bibliography," New York Bureau of Publications, Teachers College, Columbia University, 1937.

21. Mathias, Willis D., *Ideas of God and Conduct,* New York: Columbia University Press, 1943.

22. Mays, Benjamin E., *The Negro's God as Reflected in His Literature,* Boston: Chapman and Grimes, 1938.

23. McDowell, John B., "The Development of the Idea of God in the Catholic Child," *Education Research Monthly,* The Catholic University of America, 1952.

24. Piaget, Jean, *The Language and Thought of the Child,* International Library of Psychology, 1925.

25. Patton, Kenneth Leo, *The Working Concepts of God Held by Young People of a Rural Community,* Typewritten A. M. Thesis, University of Chicago, 1939.

26. Roloff, Else, "Vom religiösen Leben der Kinder," *Arch. für Religionspsychologie* (Tübingen, 1921), 2—3, 190—203.

27. Rosser, Pearl, *Your Child Grows Toward God,* Philadelphia: The Judson Press, 1945 (Pamphlet).

28. Schmieding, A., *Understanding the Child,* St. Louis: Concordia Publishing House, 1945.

29. Smith, J. J., "Religious Development in Children," *Child Psychology,* ed. Skinner and Harriman, New York: Macmillan Co., 1941.

30. Starbuck, Edwin D., *Psychology of Religion,* New York: Charles Scribner's Sons, 1900.

31. Stunk, Orlo, Jr., ed., *Readings in the Psychology of Religion,* Nashville: Abingdon Press, 1959.

32. Terman, L. M. et al., *Genetic Studies of Genius: I. Mental and Physical Traits of a Thousand Gifted Children,* Stanford University Press, 1925.

33. Watson, G. B., *The Scientific Method in Religious Education,* New York: Association Press, 1927.

34. Webster, Winifred Rachel, *The Use of Pictures in Worship for Youth,* 280 pp. Typewritten A. M. Thesis, University of Chicago, 1930.

35. West, P. V., and Skinner, C. E., *Psychology for Religious and Social Workers,* New York: D. Appleton-Century Co., 1930.

36. Wood, William Carleton, *The Dramatic Method in Religious Education,* New York: Abingdon Press, 1931.

81

APPENDIX X

Results of a Retest After Two Years

As an example of a possible Test-Retest study, there follow the verbatim responses of 19 children who were tested at the 6th and retested at the 8th grade level, using the same pictures and questions. After listing the responses for each child, a brief summary-analysis highlights the similarities and the differences in the answers given over the two-year period. There is evidence of improved concepts, of greater maturity in verbal expression in earlier than in later answers, of no change in some, of greater detail in later answers, and of mixtures of several of the above descriptions. A thorough study of the development of God-concepts in children by the longitudinal method would appear to be warranted.

VERNON

Grade 6	Grade 8
1. No answer	1. We don't know
9. Angel reminds of God He is holy	9. Angel reminds of God He is holy
10. Man is praying for forgiveness	10. Man is praying
13. Man is wrong	13. Don't know
15. God would accept the child No answer	15. God would ask all children to come to Him No answer
20. Atomic power comes from God He likes it	20. Atomic power comes from God Don't know
22. God keeps promises The Bible says so	22. God keeps promises The Bible says so
23. No answer No answer	23. God was in heaven He was making the child
27. God hates the devil	27. God disapproves of the devil
29. No answer	29. Don't know
30. No answer	30. Don't know
33. No answer	33. Don't know
35. "Yes," people would act differently Likes Picture 9 of angel Dislikes Picture 27 of devil	35. "Yes," people would act differently Likes Picture 37 of boy in dark Dislikes Picture 27 of devil

Vernon's tests are significant for the answers he does not know. On the first test there were 7 questions left blank: 1, 15b, 23a & b, 29, 30, and 33. Of these, Vernon answered only No. 23a&b in his second test, answering the res with "We don't know." Of the other answers, Nos. 9, 10, 20a, 27, and 35 were answered almost identically both times. Two questions, 20b and 13, were answered the first time but not the second. The answers Vernon does give seem to indicate that he has the right idea in regard to the concepts.

RHEA

Grade 6	Grade 8
1. God is not like old woman God is unchanging, eternal	1. God is not like old woman God is unchanging, eternal
9. Angel reminds of God Halo shows holiness, angel is over everything	9. Angel reminds of God Halo shows holiness, angel is God's helper
10. Man is praying for help to be honest and not to commit another crime	10. Man is praying He repents
13. God is greatest power	13. God is greatest power
15. God would accept older child We should love all equally	15. God would accept older child Mother should accept children equally
20. Atomic power comes from God God wants it to help man	20. No answer We should use atom for good
22. God keeps promises God has answered prayers	22. God keeps promises God is faithful
23. God was with mother and child God was protecting them	23. God was with the mother and child God was protecting the baby
27. Devil keeps people from believing	27. Devil is evil angel
29. God made man strong	29. God is stronger, man should use strength for God and man
30. Sick girl should have faith She will be rewarded in heaven	30. Parents won't worry if girl is in heaven
33. Run-aways should come home and repent	33. Boy should beg parents and God for forgiveness
35. People wouldn't be there. If they were Christians they'd feel unwanted Likes Picture 35 of happy family Dislikes Picture 27 of devil	35. People would be fighting Likes Picture 10 of man in prison Dislikes Picture 15 of mother rejecting older child

Although the above comments do not show it, Rhea's first answers were very well done. Especially noteworthy were her very perceptive comments and her command of the language. Her second answers did not seem as outstanding. As to the basic ideas represented, answers to questions 1, 9, 10, 13, 15, 20b, 22, 23, 27, 33, and 35 were similar. No. 29 was answered well, but differently both times. The second answer includes added interpretations. No. 30 was also answered well, but differently each time. The first answer shows understanding of the sick girl's feelings; the second, the parents.

JANET

Grade 6	Grade 8

1. God is not like old woman
   God is unchanging
	1. God is not like old woman
	   God is a spirit, unchanging

9. Angel reminds of God
   Halo shows cleanness and pureness
	9. Angel reminds of God
	   Angel is in heaven with God

10. Man is asking for release from prison (God's will be done)	10. Man is praying He is in a praying position
13. God is greatest power	13. God is greatest power

15. Mother should love both equally
   No answer
	15. God would show mother her wrong
	   Mother should love older child too

20. Atomic power comes from God
   It's good if used carefully
	20. Atomic power is indirectly from God
	   Man should use it wisely

22. God keeps promises
   Bible and catechism say so
	22. God keeps promises
	   He promised and sent a Savior

23. God was with the baby
   He was making it grow
	23. God was with mother and baby
	   God was helping them

27. Devil is unclean, harsh, and tricky	27. God hates the devil
29. God is stronger	29. God gave man strength God is stronger
30. If girl dies, she'll go to heaven	30. God will comfort parents, but girl should have faith
33. Run-aways are foolish, parents will forgive	33. Running away is wrong

35. "Yes," people would act differently
   Likes Picture 35 of peaceful family
   Dislikes Picture 27 of devil
	35. People wouldn't be there if God weren't there
	   Likes Picture 7 of nature scene
	   Dislikes Picture 4 of boy vowing to keep a secret

Janet's answers to her second test sometimes showed clearer understanding and sometimes less understanding of the concepts than in her first answers. Nos. 10 and 33 are answered with more insight the first time. Nos. 15, 20, 29, and 35 revealed more insight in the second answers. Other questions, though answered differently, show a good understanding both times. (Nos. 1, 9, 22, 23, 27, and 30.)

ANNE

Grade 6	Grade 8

1. God is not like old woman
   God is unchanging
	1. God is not old like woman
	   God is unchanging

9. Angel reminds of God
   Angel is holy
	9. Angel reminds of God
	   Both are holy

10. Man is praying for forgiveness	10. Man is praying, he is sorry

84

13. It isn't greatest power
15. God would treat mother like the child (punish? exclude?) Both children are equal
20. Atomic power comes from God God disapproves
22. God keeps promises God answers prayer
23. God was with the baby He was taking care of it
27. Devil is bad to everyone
29. God gave man his strength
30. Sick girl shouldn't worry about parents
33. Run-away should ask forgiveness
35. "Yes," people would act differently Likes Picture 9 of angel Dislikes Picture 15 of mother rejecting child

13. Man is not telling the truth
15. God would tell mother her mistake She should love both children
20. Atomic power comes from God Bible doesn't tell about it
22. God keeps promises Bible says so
23. God was with the mother and baby Creating baby, protecting mother
27. God is angry with the devil
29. God gave man his strength
30. God will care for parents
33. Running away is wrong
35. "Yes," people would act differently Likes Picture 9 of angel Dislikes Picture 27 of devil

Though she answered each question differently, Anne expressed the same ideas throughout the tests. It would be difficult to show that her second set of questions showed any change in understanding the concepts. The answer to No. 15 of the first test is the only statement that stands out to any degree.

KARLA

Grade 6

1. God is not like woman God is a spirit
9. Angel does not remind of God God is a spirit

10. Man in prison is praying

13. God knows man is wrong, so does man
15. God would accept child Mother should love both
20. Atomic power comes from God God must think it is good since He gave it to man
22. God keeps promises He promised and sent a Savior

Grade 8

1. God is not like woman God is eternal
9. Angel does remind of God Angel is sinless, God's helper Angel does not remind of God God is almighty, angel only helper

10. Man in prison is praying He is sorry for his sins

13. Man is wrong, God is greatest

15. God would love both equally Mother should love both
20. Atomic power comes from God It is good if it helps man
22. God keeps promises He promised and sent a Savior

23. God was protecting mother	23. God was protecting the child
Same answer	God was giving mother strength and protecting the child
27. Devil is source of all sin	27. God hates sin and devil, yet loves everyone
29. God gave man strength	29. God loves man, but man must use his strength for good
30. Girl will go to heaven	30. Girl should not worry
33. Run-away is doing wrong	33. Run-away resents his parents, is spoiled, wants own way
35. People would not behave differently	35. People would behave differently
Likes Picture 22 of father giving son a bike	Likes Picture 35 of peaceful family
Dislikes Picture 15 of mother rejecting child	Dislikes Picture 5 of boy in court

Karla's answers remained basically the same during the two-year period, but she answered in more detail and often showed increased understanding on the second test. Especially noticeable is her command and use of words in 8th grade (see Nos. 20, 23, and 33). These answers also show a good deal of insight. Karla's increased knowledge seemed to interfere and cause unsureness in No. 27.

JUDY

Grade 6	Grade 8
1. God is not like old woman	1. God is not like old woman
No answer	God is unchanging
9. Angel reminds of God	9. Angel reminds of God
Angel is in heaven	Angel looks like God
10. Man is praying for forgiveness	10. Man is praying for forgiveness
13. Man is showing off, may hurt someone	13. God is greatest power
15. No answer	15. God would accept both children
Mother is pushing child away	God would say, "Come to Me"
20. No answer	20. No answer
No answer	No answer
22. God keeps promises	22. God keeps promises
God promised boy in picture a bike	Promised and sent a Savior
23. No answer	23. God was caring for mother and child
God was caring for mother and child	God was caring for mother and child
27. God thinks the devil is terrible	27. God thinks the devil is terrible
29. No answer	29. God is greatest power
30. Sick girl will not die	30. Sick girl will not die
33. Run-away will be punished (harmed)	33. Run-away should be good

35. "No," people wouldn't act
    differently
    Likes Pictures 9, 16, 22, 23, and 6
    Dislikes Pictures 13, 17, 20, 27, 28,
    30, 32, 34, 36

35. "No," people wouldn't act
    differently
    Likes Picture 9 of angel
    Dislikes Picture 27 of devil

Judy's second group of answers showed a slight increase in understanding of the concepts involved. She added the ideas that God is unchanging (No. 1), God is the greatest power (No. 13, 29), and showed an increased understanding of God's accepting all children (No. 15), and God's keeping a promise in sending His Son (No. 22). Answers to questions 9, 10, 22, 23, 27, 30, 33, and 35 were basically the same or only slightly different. Judy apparently did not understand the concept of the question about atomic power either time.

HARLAN

Grade 6

1. God is not old like woman
   He is a spirit, eternal
9. Angel reminds of God
   Both are sinless
10. Man in prison is praying

13. God does not like what man says

15. God would make older child get
    sick (punishment? or to give
    child chance for attention?)
20. Atomic power comes from God
    No answer
22. God keeps promises
    No answer
23. God was with the mother
    He was making the baby grow
27. God hates the devil
29. No answer

30. Sick girl should have faith
33. Run-away should repent
35. "Yes," people would behave
    differently
    Likes Picture 9 of angel
    Dislikes Picture 27 of devil

Grade 8

1. God is not old like woman
   He is unchanging
9. Angel reminds of God
   It is holy
10. Man in prison is praying
    He wishes to be forgiven
13. Man is not telling truth
    God makes the chemicals
15. God would treat children equally
    "Everyone is equal"

20. Atomic power comes from God
    It is good if used right
22. God does keep promises
    God gives us what is good for us
23. God was helping the baby grow
    He was protecting the mother
27. God thinks devil is bad
29. Man should use his strength for
    God
30. God will help sick girl
33. Run-away will be found
35. "Yes," they would argue and fight
    Likes Pictures 9 of angel
    Dislikes Picture 27 of devil

Harlan's answers to the retest questions show no important change from his first answers, except that he feels more able to answer two "why" questions and another question ignored entirely the first time (Nos. 20, 22, and 29).

I thought the answer to No. 15 was unusual and worth noting, also the answer to No. 33.

CAROL

Grade 6	Grade 8
1. Don't know Never saw God	1. No God is eternal
9. Yes Holy reminds of God	9. Yes Holy reminds of God
10. Praying	10. Praying Is sorry
13. No answer	13. God knows all things
15. God would accept all God would love both	15. God would love both God would love both
20. Atomic power comes from God God thinks it is bad	20. Atomic power comes from God God gave it to man
22. God keeps promises Don't know	22. God keeps promises God is perfect, doesn't sin
23. God was with mother and child Don't know what he was doing	23. God was with mother and child He was protecting them
27. God thinks devil is evil	27. God hates the devil
29. Don't know	29. God gave man strength to use for good
30. Sick girl will not die	30. Sick girl should not worry God will care for her
33. Running away won't help	33. God feels sorry for run-away
35. People would act differently Likes Picture 9 of angel best Dislikes Picture 27 of devil	35. People might act differently Likes Picture 9 of angel best Dislikes Picture 27 of devil

Carol's answers changed significantly in two years, showing in most cases a clearer understanding of the concepts. In 6th grade she stated frequently that she did not know (Nos. 1, 13, 22, 23, and 29), thus showing that she was afraid or unwilling to even try to answer the questions. When she took the retest in eighth grade, Carol answered all these questions and in every case seemed to show a clear understanding of the concept. There were only 3 questions which had the same answers both times (Nos. 9, 15, 27). Of the remaining questions, 10, 20, 30, and 33 were answered better the second time. No. 35 showed a growing unsureness.

DICK

Grade 6	Grade 8
1. God is not like old woman God is a spirit, triune	1. God is not like old woman God is never idle
9. Angel reminds of God Is God's holy messenger	9. Angel reminds of God Is pure and holy like God

88

10. Man in prison is praying

13. Man should not forget to think of God

15. God would tell mother not to push child aside
Same answer

20. Atomic power comes from God
It is bad, destroys people

22. God keeps promises
Literature says so

23. God was helping the baby
He was nursing it

27. God thinks devil is evil

29. Strong man has developed the body God gave him

30. Sick girl will be with parents in heaven

33. Run-away should ask forgiveness

35. "Yes," people would behave differently
Likes Picture 38 of poor boys
Dislikes Picture 5 of boy in court

---

10. Man in prison is praying
He wants to be forgiven

13. Man does not know about God

15. God would accept the child
He would say, "Come little children"

20. Atomic power comes indirectly from God. His power is greatest

22. God keeps promises
He says he does

23. God was inside the mother
He guarded the reproductive procedure

27. Devil is sinful and unholy

29. God is stronger than the strong man

30. God will help the sick girl

33. Run-away should be forgiven if he is sorry

35. "Yes," people would behave differently
Likes Picture 35 of family group
Dislikes Picture 17 of boy declaring hate

DONALD

Grade 6

1. Don't know if God is like woman
Has never seen God

9. Angel reminds of God
God is holy

10. Man in prison is praying

13. If man was thinking bad things, he would be sinning

15. God would accept older child
God would accept older child

20. Atomic power comes from God
It is bad if used wrong

22. God keeps promises
He promised and sent a Savior

Grade 8

1. God is not like old woman
God is eternal

9. Angel reminds of God
God is holy

10. Man in prison is praying
He might be sorry

13. "No"

15. God would help
He would love all equally

20. Atomic power comes from God
It is good if we use it right

22. God keeps promises
He promised and sent a Savior

89

23. God was in heaven He was watching everyone	23. God was with the mother He was helping her
27. God thinks the devil is evil	27. God doesn't like the devil
29. The strong man is good if he is a Christian	29. The strong man is good if he is a Christian
30. The sick girl should trust God	30. The girl won't die
33. Run-away should turn to God	33. Run-away should stay home
35. "No," if they were Christians (people would not act differently) Likes Picture 9 of angel Dislikes Picture 27 of the devil	35. "Yes," people would act differently Likes Picture 10 of man praying in prison Dislikes Picture 27 of the devil

Donald's answers show no clear-cut trend when the test answers are compared. Seven of the 13 pairs of answers studied remained the same or nearly the same (Nos. 9, 10, 15, 20, 22, 27, and 29). The most significant change occurred in No. 1, where an "I don't know" answer was replaced by an understanding of God's eternal quality. In No. 23, Donald limits his answer from "God is watching everyone," to specify that God was with the mother. Neither of the answers to No. 13 is clear, but the child seems to have at least a little understanding of the concept. Despite the two different answers to No. 35, it seems that Donald understands what the question is seeking to learn.

JUDY

Grade 6	Grade 8
1. God is not like old woman God is unchanging	1. God is not like old woman God is a spirit, eternal
9. Angel reminds of God God is holy Angel doesn't remind of God Angel has wings	9. Angel reminds of God God is holy Angel doesn't remind of God God is a spirit without body
10. Man is praying for forgiveness	10. Man is praying He is sorry
13. Man worships chemistry, not God	13. God is greatest power
15. No answer Mother should love both children	15. Mother should love both equally Mother should love both equally
20. Atomic power comes from "atomic energy and minerals" Man put this before God	20. Atomic power comes from God Shouldn't be used for harm
22. God keeps promises Promise about no flood to Noah	22. God keeps promises Promised Noah would never send flood
23. No answer No answer	23. God was with the baby He was helping it grow

27. Devil is evil, tries to make people sin

27. Devil is evil, tries to make people sin
We should obey God

29. Man might worship strength before God

29. Man should use strength for good, not show off

30. Girl shouldn't be afraid to die

30. God will make sick girl well

33. Run-away should return and repent

33. Run-away should not run away and grieve parents

35. "Yes," people would act differently
Likes Picture 9 of angel
Dislikes Picture 27 of devil

35. "Yes," people would act differently
Likes Picture 23 of mother and child
Dislikes Picture 20 of atom bomb

Judy's second answers show increased understanding of the concepts involved. Nos. 13, 20a&b, 23a&b show much clearer understanding in the second answers. The change in No. 29 is not as great, but it is an improvement. No. 30 reveals a change in attitude from expectation of the girl's death to assurance she will not die. No. 9 is answered both positively and negatively each time. Nos. 1, 9, 10, 15, 22, 27, and 35 were answered similarly in each test.

DARLENE

Grade 6

1. God is like old woman
He is busy, like she is sewing
9. Angel reminds of God
God has halo
Angel does not remind of God
God doesn't have wings
10. "He done wrong" (man in prison)

13. God is greatest power
15. God would take the child away
He would tell mother to love the other child, too
20. Atomic power is from God
God is greatest power

22. God keeps promises
He promised and sent a Savior
23. God was in the mother
He was making the baby healthy
27. "The people" (inappropriate)
29. God is stronger
30. Sick girl will get well
33. God is angry, but forgives

Grade 8

1. God is not like old woman
God is busy
9. Angel reminds of God
God is holy

10. Man is praying (paying for his mistake)
13. God is angry, man is wrong
15. God would care for both. He would tell children to come to Him

20. Atomic power is from God (atoms)
We can't know what God thinks √
22. God keeps promises
He promised and sent a Savior
23. God was in the mother
He was making the baby
27. Can't know what God thinks √
29. God made man strong
30. Sick girl will get well √
33. God is angry, but forgives √

91

35. "Yes," people would act differently
    Likes Picture 6 of nature scene
    Dislikes Picture 5 of boy in court

35. "Yes," people would act differently
    Likes Picture 22 of father giving
    bike to boy
    Dislikes Picture 32 of rich man

The most significant thing in Darlene's tests is the strange attitude shown on the second test. She repeatedly states that she cannot say what God would do, think, or say, because "I don't know, I'm not holy." (The check marks (√) indicate this on the remarks above.) Her attitude is almost impudent, because she often adds this statement after she gives a good answer to the question. Otherwise, questions 20, 22, 23, 30, 33, and 35 are answered similarly both times. No. 1 shows a conflict. One answer says God is like the old woman because she is busy, the other says He is not like the old woman because she is idle. Darlene answers the 9th question both negatively and positively on the first test.

KEITH

Grade 6

1. God is not like old woman
   God is almighty, eternal
9. Angel reminds of God
   Is praying, guarding a sinner
10. Man is praying for forgiveness
13. God is greatest power
    Man is wrong
15. God would tell mother not to push
    child away
    God would ask children to come
20. Atomic power comes from God
    He doesn't approve
22. God keeps promises
    He promised and sent His Son
23. God was in the mother
    He was making the baby grow
27. God disapproves of devil
29. God is stronger
30. Sick girl shouldn't worry
33. Run-away should face his wrong
    doing
35. "Yes," people would act differently
    Likes Picture 23 of mother and
    baby
    Dislikes Picture 28 of boys robbing
    jewelry store

Grade 8

1. God is old like woman
   God is old like woman
9. Angel reminds of God
   God is pure and holy
10. Man is praying for forgiveness
13. God is greatest power
15. God would take the child
    God would ask children to come to
    Him
20. Atomic power comes from atoms
    It could be used better
22. God keeps promises
    He said He would
23. God was everywhere
    He was doing everything
27. Devil is God's enemy
29. God is stronger
30. Sick girl shouldn't worry
33. Run-away should feel sorry
35. "No," people would not act
    differently
    Likes Picture 9 of angel
    Dislikes Picture 27 of devil

With a few exceptions, Keith answered the second set of questions like he did the first. Questions 9, 10, 13, 15 b, 22, 27, 29, and 30 are answered similarly both times. But the added details of 9, 15a, 22b, are different, showing neither increased nor decreased understanding of the concepts. Answers to Questions 1, 20, 23, and 35 are answered completely opposite the second time, but the first answers were a more correct understanding of the concepts.

MARY ANN

Grade 6	Grade 8
1. God is not like old woman God is eternal	1. God is not like old woman God is eternal
9. Angel reminds of God Is with God, holy like God	9. Angel reminds of God Is holy like God
10. Man is praying for forgiveness	10. Man is praying He is repentant
13. God is greatest power	13. Man is not telling truth
15. God would accept the older child God would tell mother to accept older child	15. God would comfort the child Mother should love both equally
20. Atomic power comes from God God is greatest power	20. Atomic power comes from God No answer
22. God keeps promises Bible says so	22. God keeps promises He says so
23. God was with the mother God was helping the mother	23. God was with mother and child God was giving the child life
27. No answer	27. Devil is God's rival
29. God loves strong man like everyone	29. God is stronger
30. Girl shouldn't worry about dying She just has the mumps	30. God would comfort sick girl
33. Running away is foolish	33. Run-away can't escape from God
35. "Yes," people would act differently Likes Picture 7 of nature scene Dislikes Picture 38 of poor boys	35. "Yes," people would act differently Likes Picture 23 of mother and child Dislikes Picture 20 of atom bomb

Mary Ann's answers were very similar for both tests, except for a few exceptions. The most interesting of these was her answer to No. 30, when she said the sick girl shouldn't worry about dying because she only had the mumps. Her second answer is prosaic compared with that. Mary Ann did not answer the question about the devil the first time (No. 27), so her second answer showed improvement. She added the idea that run-aways can't escape from God in her second answer to No. 33. The rest of her answers employed similar ideas each time.

LARRY

Grade 6	Grade 8
1. God is not like old woman God is unchanging	1. God is not like old woman God is unchanging

9. Angel reminds of God
   Is angel of God
   Angel doesn't remind of God
   God is brighter, more glorious
10. Man is praying for forgiveness
13. God is greatest power
15. God would make child happy
20. Atomic power comes from God
    If it's used right, it's good; if not, bad
22. God keeps promises
    Boy in picture got his bike
23. God was in heaven
    He was taking care of the mother
27. Devil is evil
29. God gave man strength
    God is more powerful
30. Sick girl will go to heaven
33. Run-away needs help to have faith
35. "Yes," people would act differently
    Likes Pictures 9, 10 of angel and man in prison
    Dislikes Pictures 27 and 38 of devil and poor boys

9. Angel reminds of God
   Angel is symbol of God, like all drawings
10. Man is repenting of his sin
13. God is greatest power
15. Don't push children away
20. Atomic power comes from God
    All right, if used for God
22. God keeps promises
    He always has and Bible says so
23. God was with the baby
    He was protecting it
27. Devil is sinful
29. God gave man strength

30. Sick girl shouldn't be afraid
33. Run-away needs help
35. "Yes," people would act differently
    Likes Picture 7 of nature scene
    Dislikes Picture 38 of poor boys

Although Larry's answers remained much the same both times, one question in the second group showed a clearer understanding. This was No. 9, which he answered both "yes" and "no" the first time. (His answers reveal a good deal of insight, nevertheless.) But his second answer expressed the idea that all drawings were but symbols of God. His other answers showed good understanding the first time and were little changed the second time. Larry stresses the fact that a run-away child needs help. (No. 33)

FREDERICK

Grade 6

1. No answer
   Don't know
9. Angel reminds of God
   Angel is holy
10. Man is praying for forgiveness
13. God doesn't like what the man is saying
15. No answer
    Mother is doing wrong

Grade 8

1. God is not like old woman
   God never changes
9. Angel reminds of God
   Angel is holy
10. Man is praying
13. Man is wrong

15. God would love older child, too
    God would ask child to come to Him

20. Atomic power comes from God
God doesn't like it

20. Atomic power comes from God
God doesn't like atomic power, He likes it the way it is

22. God keeps promises
If you keep promises, He will too

22. God keeps promises
God answers prayer

23. No answer
God was keeping baby safe

23. God was with mother and child
God made the baby

27. God doesn't like the devil

27. God doesn't like the devil

29. No answer

29. God loves the strong man

30. Sick girl shouldn't worry

30. Sick girl shouldn't worry

33. God doesn't like run-aways

33. God doesn't like run-aways

35. God is there!
Likes Picture 9 of angel
Dislikes Picture 27 of devil

35. "Yes," people would act differently
Likes Picture 23 of mother and baby
Dislikes Picture 27 of devil

Frederick's second group of answers showed a slight improvement over his understanding as shown by his first answers. He left 4 questions blank the first time, 1a, 15a, 23a, and 29 but he answered all the questions the second time. The rest of his answers were similar to (some exactly like) his first answers. Answers to 15b, 22b, and 35 were almost the only ones that differed. Frederick's answer to No. 20b is rather difficult to understand.

JUDY

Grade 6

1. God is not like old woman
God is unchanging

9. Angel reminds of God
Angel works with and for God

10. Man is praying for forgiveness

13. The man is right

15. God would love both children
God would love both children

20. Atomic power comes from God
Sometimes it's all right

22. God keeps promises
God is sinless

23. God was with the baby
God was protecting the baby

27. Devil is sinful, takes people to hell

29. Man is no better than anyone else

30. Sick girl will get well, be saved

33. Run-away is wrong, should repent

Grade 8

1. God is not like old woman
God is eternal

9. Angel reminds of God
Reminds of holy being

10. Man is praying for forgiveness

13. God is greatest power

15. God would love both children
God would love both children

20. Atomic power comes from man
All right if used for good

22. God keeps promises
Past experience, Bible, sent Savior

23. God was with the baby
God was protecting the baby

27. God despises devil, is evil

29. God gave man strength

30. Sick girl will get well, if she believes

33. Running away is wrong
He should realize his mistake

95

35. "No," people wouldn't act differently
    Likes Picture 23 of mother and child
    Dislikes Picture 27 of devil

35. "Yes," people would act differently
    Likes Pictures 8, 6, and 7 of nature scenes and boy apologizing for pushing
    Dislikes Pictures 27 and 28 of devil and boys robbing store

Judy's answers to Nos. 13, 20, and 35 were startlingly different. Her first answer to No. 13 says that the chemical is the greatest power, the second says God is. Her first answer to 20 says God made atomic power, the second says man did. No. 35's "no" answer was changed to a "yes." Her first answer to No. 29, that the strong man was no better than anyone else, was changed later to say that God gave the man his strength. Otherwise, the answers to Nos. 1, 9, 10, 15, 22, 23, 27, 30, and 33 were similar both times.

PAULINE

Grade 6

1. God is not like old woman
   God is eternal

9. Angel reminds of God
   Angel is holy

10. Man is sorry for doing wrong

13. God doesn't like what man says

15. God would make mother love child
    Mother should love everyone

20. Atomic power comes from God
    It could be used to destroy

22. God keeps promises
    God never sins

23. God was with mother and everyone
    God was helping mother

27. God will put devil in hell

29. God loves strong man

30. Parents will be sad

33. God will help run-away return home

35. "Yes," people would act differently
    Likes Pictures 35 and 9 of happy family and of angel
    Dislikes Pictures 27 and 28 of devil and boys robbing jewelry store

Grade 8

1. God is not like old woman
   God is eternal

9. Angel doesn't remind of God
   Don't know what God looks like

10. Man is praying for God's help

13. Man is not telling truth

15. God wouldn't like what mother did
    Mother should love both

20. Atomic power comes from God
    Don't know what God thinks

22. God keeps promises
    Bible says so

23. God was everywhere
    God was helping baby grow

27. God dislikes devil

29. God gave man his strength

30. Everything will be all right

33. God doesn't like running away

35. "Yes," people would act differently
    Likes Picture 23 of mother and child
    Dislikes Picture 17 of boy declaring hate

Although Pauline's answers were different almost every time, it is difficult to determine any clear or definite trend. The most noticeable changes occurred in No. 9 and 20, where the questions were answered very satisfactorily the first time, but answered with "I don't know what God looks like — or thinks," the second time.

GARY

<table>
<tr><td colspan="2" align="center">Grade 6</td><td colspan="2" align="center">Grade 8</td></tr>
<tr><td>1.</td><td>God is not like old woman
God is a spirit</td><td>1.</td><td>God is not like old woman
God is unchanging</td></tr>
<tr><td>9.</td><td>Angel doesn't remind of God
Angel isn't a spirit</td><td>9.</td><td>Angel doesn't remind of God
God is spirit</td></tr>
<tr><td>10.</td><td>Man is praying for forgiveness</td><td>10.</td><td>Man is praying for forgiveness</td></tr>
<tr><td>13.</td><td>Man is wrong
God is greatest power</td><td>13.</td><td>God is greatest power</td></tr>
<tr><td>15.</td><td>No answer
No answer</td><td>15.</td><td>God would disapprove of mother
We should love everyone</td></tr>
<tr><td>20.</td><td>Atomic power comes from God
God doesn't like it</td><td>20.</td><td>Atomic power comes from the
atom
God's power is greater</td></tr>
<tr><td>22.</td><td>God keeps promises
God doesn't lie</td><td>22.</td><td>God keeps promises
God is faithful</td></tr>
<tr><td>23.</td><td>God was with the mother
He was helping her</td><td>23.</td><td>God was everywhere
He was ruling heaven and earth</td></tr>
<tr><td>27.</td><td>God dislikes the devil</td><td>27.</td><td>God hates the devil</td></tr>
<tr><td>29.</td><td>God gave man strength</td><td>29.</td><td>God is stronger</td></tr>
<tr><td>30.</td><td>Girl cannot know future</td><td>30.</td><td>Girl shouldn't worry about future</td></tr>
<tr><td>33.</td><td>No answer</td><td>33.</td><td>Children should obey parents</td></tr>
<tr><td>35.</td><td>"Yes," people would act differently
Likes Picture 8 of boy apologizing
for pushing
Dislikes Picture 27 of devil</td><td>35.</td><td>"Yes," people would act differently
Likes Picture 8 of boy apologizing
for pushing
Dislikes Picture 27 of devil</td></tr>
</table>

Some increase in understanding is shown in Gary's second group of answers. This is most clearly seen in Nos. 15 and 33, which Gary did not answer at all the first time. He has an unusual concept of why the angel is not remindful of God. No. 9 seems to show that he thinks God is a spirit, but an angel is not. Gary stresses the point of not worrying about the future (No. 30). Although he says that atomic power comes from the atom rather than God on his second answer (No. 20), Gary does not deny the fact that God has all power. The rest of his answers showed little change.

Categorizing Key

1. 0. God as God, eternal, never changing
   1. God — powerful
   2. God, not human
   3. Man, anthropomorphism
   4. Authority, Bible, priest, minister
   5. Not certain; don't know
   6. Inappropriate. God is male
   7. Yes
   8. No
   9. No answer

2. 0. Omnipresence
   1. Omnipotence
   2. Omniscience
   3. Inappropriate
   4. No
   5. Don't know
   6. Yes, miscellaneous
   9. No answer

3. 0. Omnipresence
   1. Omnipotent
   2. God in another world
   3. He is in heaven
   4. He is in this world
   5. Don't know
   6. Inappropriate
   7. No
   8. Yes
   9. No answer

4. 0. Omniscience
   1. No
   2. Yes
   9. No answer

5. 0. God thinks he should repent
   1. God feels sorry for him
   2. God will forgive him
   3. God thinks he is a sinner, bad
   4. He should be punished
   5. Miscellaneous — it depends. God loves him; don't know.
   6. No answer
   7. Yes
   8. No
   9. Yes, if he doesn't repent

6. 0. God
   1. Nature
   2. Inappropriate
   3. Don't know
   9. No answer

7. 0. God made it that way
   1. Don't know
   2. Nature
   3. Inappropriate
   9. No answer

8. 0. God is happy he said he was sorry
   1. He thinks the boy is nice; good sport
   2. He will forgive him
   3. He thinks he shouldn't hav/ pushed him
   4. God dislikes him
   5. Don't know
   6. Miscellaneous
   9. No answer

9. 0. Yes. Angels are in heaven where God is Holy
   1. Yes. Physical likeness. Holy reminds of God
   2. Yes. Relationship implied (It is praying)
   3. Yes. Reminded of divine qualities of God
   4. No. God is a spirit

5. Yes
6. Don't know how God looks
7. God was not created
9. No answer

10. 0. Praying for forgiveness. Reads Bible
    1. Merely praying
    2. Serving prison sentence
    3. Pray — help get out of prison
    4. Help lead clean life when released
    5. Pray for God's help
    6. Inappropriate
    9. No answer

11. 0. No
    1. No. He never dies
    2. No. It says so in the Bible
    3. Yes
    4. Yes, if he wants to
    5. Anthropomorphism
    6. God is spirit or God is Creator
    7. Don't know
    9. No answer

12. 0. No
    1. No, God is always with us, everywhere
    2. No, miscellaneous
    3. Yes
    9. No answer

13. 0. He is wrong; God is greatest power
    1. He is wrong, boasting
    2. The man is right
    3. He doesn't like it
    4. He is not a Christian
    5. He shouldn't — danger!
    6. He doesn't know about God
    7. Thank God for power
    8. Inappropriate
    9. No answer

14. 0. Yes
    1. No
    2. No answer
    3. Yes
    4. No

5. Inappropriate
9. No answer

15. 0. God would accept older (all) child(ren)
    1. God would make the mother suffer
    2. No response
    3. She should love all equally
    4. Come here, My son
    5. He does not like her; is disappointed
    6. Golden rule
    7. Man is selfish
    8. Mother must take care of the baby
    9. No response

16. 0. Yes
    1. He created them
    2. He takes care of them
    3. No
    4. They do not have souls
    9. No answer

17. 0. Reconciliation or sharing
    1. Mere statement of facts
    2. God forgives; does not hate
    3. Hate is like murder
    4. Differing religions produce fighting
    5. God does not like hating
    6. "I hate" — something happens
    7. Inappropriate
    9. No answer

18. 0. God has human nature; God, divine
    1. God put on humanity in Christ
    2. God is always kind
    3. No response. Don't know
    4. God is holy, wise — man is sinful
    5. God is not limited by a body
    6. God will not die
    7. Anthropomorphism
    8. God can work miracles — man can't
    9. No response

19. 0. Yes
    1. No

99

2. Omnipotent
3. Omnipresence
4. From the Bible
5. Statement of fact or belief
6. Inappropriate
9. No answer

20. 0. God
1. From the ground; natural causes
2. No answer
3. God thinks He wants it this way
4. God thinks well of it; it's good
5. God thinks it is *not* good
6. God thinks He is greater than atom power
7. We don't know
8. Good if helps man; evil if harms man
9. No answer

21. 0. Yes
1. No
2. No answer
3. Omniscience
4. Omnipresence
5. Man needs help
6. Humanity of God
7. Inappropriate
9. No answer

22. 0. Yes
1. No
2. Not always
3. No answer
4. God is truthful
5. God never fails
6. God keeps promise. — Bible
7. Experience — has kept promise
8. God has to help others
9. No answer

23. 0. God was everywhere
1. God was with the mother and/or child
2. God was in heaven
3. God was in the baby
4. God was giving her a baby; a blessing
5. God was developing the baby

6. God was giving her faith
7. Inappropriate
8. Don't know
9. No response

24. 0. Why aren't you careful?
1. You are a bad girl; Mother scolds her
2. No answer
3. Why didn't you ask me?
4. Forgive her; tell her not to repeat it
5. Pick them up and put them away
6. You shouldn't do such things
7. It is a sin. He would finish
8. Obey your parents
9. No answer or Don't know

25. 0. Yes
1. No
2. No answer
3. God is eternal
4. Bible tells us he won't die
5. My minister, priest, rabbi told me
6. Inappropriate
7. He died on the cross
8. God is a spirit
9. No response

26. 0. Yes
1. No
2. No answer

27. 0. God thinks devils are bad; doesn't like devil
1. Devil should be punished
2. Devil is not very nice
3. He hates the devil
4. Inappropriate
5. God is greater than the devil
6. Keeps people from believing
7. Should obey God, not devil
8. Don't know and Miscellaneous
9. No answer

28. 0. Yes
1. No
2. No answer
3. Omniscience

100

4. They're stealing
5. Omnipresent
6. All power
9. No answer

29. 0. God is stronger
1. Observation of fact; a strong man
2. Don't know
3. This one is not the only strong man on earth
4. God wants him to use his strength to work for God
5. God loves him. He's O. K.
6. God gave him strength
7. He is a sinner
8. Miscellaneous
9. No answer

30. 0. You will not die
1. Believe on Jesus and be saved
2. I will make you well
3. Your parents would feel bad but they could get along without you
4. God will let her find out
5. You are in My hand; pray: protection
6. You will meet your father and mother in heaven
7. They would be very happy
8. Don't know
9. No answer

31. 0. Yes
1. No
2. No answer
3. He is everlasting — or many
4. Nobody knows
5. He had a birthday at Christmas
6. He is different
7. 30—32
8. None
9. No answer

32. 0. He is greedy — selfish
1. It is not true; God helped him
2. He is disobeying the 1st Commandment
3. Stealing
4. He is rich

5. Give to church
6. Inappropriate
7. God will punish
8. Don't know
9. No answer

33. 0. He is not loyal
1. It is a sin
2. It is wrong; he shouldn't do it
3. He should face up to it and take the consequences
4. God would give him a beating
5. He misunderstood his parents and should stay there
6. He is running away from God
7. Don't know
8. Inappropriate
9. No answer

34. 0. Yes
1. No
2. Boy is bad and God can't do anything
3. God had already tried to help him
4. No answer
5. By making the driver stop the car or boy stops
6. By telling him to watch for cars
7. Don't know
8. If God thought best, would help; God can do anything
9. No answer

35. 0. Yes
1. No
2. Not known
3. It depends
4. People not living or in existence
9. No answer

36. 0. Bad. Scared. Lonesome
1. Scared but God is with me
2. I feel good, fine
3. God is helping the farmers
4. God is nearer to me
5. Not known
6. No difference
7. Sad — can't go out

101

8. It depends; miscellaneous
9. No answer
37. 0. Assurance by personal presence
"I am with you: don't be afraid"
1. He should go home
2. Don't know
9. No answer
38. 0. Bad, sorry, sad
1. Happy
2. Same as if he were in heaven

3. Displeased — "clean up this mess"
4. God would help them
5. You should have a better life
6. Equality before God
7. Don't know or, nothing
8. Inappropriate, misunderstood the question
9. No answer

39. Picture liked most:
40. Picture liked least:

APPENDIX Z

THE KEY TO CONTROL ITEMS

Column on
IBM card: 5   41. Mental level:

0. 140+
1. 130—139 very high
2. 120—129 high
3. 110—119 high average
4. 100—109 average
5. 90—99   low average
6. 80—89   low
7. 70—79   very low

Col. 6   42. School:

0. public
1. Lutheran
2. Catholic
3. other private

Col. 7   43. Grade:

0. pre-school
1. 1st grade
2. 2d grade
      etc.

Col. 8   44. State:

0. Indiana
1. Illinois
2. Michigan
3. Wisconsin

Col. 9   45. Sex:

0. boy
1. girl

Col. 10   46. Age: 0. pre-school
                                             1. 6.
                                             2. 7.
                                             3. 8.
                                             4. 9.
                                             5. 10.
                                             6. 11.
                                             7. 12.
                                             8. 13.
                                             9. 14.

Col. 11   47. Children   0.
                     in family: 1. 1.
                                             2. 2.
                                                etc.